A PHENOMENOLOGY OF LANGERIAN MINDFULNESS

A PHENOMENOLOGY OF LANGERIAN MINDFULNESS

The Psychology of Presence

Sayyed Mohsen Fatemi

LEXINGTON BOOKS
Lanham • Boulder • New York • London

Published by Lexington Books
An imprint of The Rowman & Littlefield Publishing Group, Inc.
4501 Forbes Boulevard, Suite 200, Lanham, Maryland 20706
www.rowman.com

Unit A, Whitacre Mews, 26-34 Stannary Street, London SE11 4AB

British Library Cataloguing in Publication Information Available

Library of Congress Cataloging-in-Publication Data Available

LCCN: 2018949700 | ISBN 9781498574228 (hardback : alk. paper) | ISBN 9781498574235 (electronic)

∞™ The paper used in this publication meets the minimum requirements of American National Standard for Information Sciences Permanence of Paper for Printed Library Materials, ANSI/NISO Z39.48-1992.

Printed in the United States of America

CONTENTS

PREFACE

Presence may serve as a key ingredient for liveliness, vivacity, and ebullience. Without presence, the connections are lost, the significance of sensibility is missing, and the realms of beings are pushed to be acting in a mechanical, robotic, and automatic manner.

When presence is there, the potential faculties of one's beings are apt to operate openly where the possibility of growth and development may enhance their horizons of actualization.

With the replacement of absence, attention ceases to operate: Not noticing the plethora of manifold possibilities, multifarious capacities, and sundry avenues of creational opportunities are easily exposed to oblivion.

Absence engenders fragmentation and fragmentation would impede the process of implementing wholeness. The whole goes away when absence steps in. A growth of fragmentation would espouse multiplicities where attention, belongings, and beings become scattered and lose their focus. You can be physically present and psychologically absent.

The sovereignty of multiplicities would encourage a disengagement from an experimental confrontation with one's presence both in subjective and objective terms.

The distance between one's knowledge of presence and one's inner and outer engagements may give rise to increasing gaps in the unified cognitive, emotional, and behavioral performance thus excluding the gift of observation in observing the possible synergy of the brain and the mind with two beings different from one another as far as the intentionality of this manuscript is concerned.

Presence may entail an intimate relationship with one's self comfortably, deliberately, and attentively. Presence oriented intimacy facilitates the process of being in touch with one's beings beyond the subjective levels of accumulated cognitive and emotional schemas.

The mere lingering in the subjective level of engagements would gradually keep one away from a communication with the true manifestation of being in the moment.

The here and now is becoming replete with back and forth references of subjective flow of images, memories, concepts, categories, recollections, and judgements.

The huge inundation of the ever increasing subjective levels of beings would push one into a world separate from the world of the present moment.

Absence galvanizes the subjective engagements and forcibly implements the disembarkation from the flow of the present moment.

As fragmentation, multiplicity, and absence marshal their disempowering power, one's presence is lost in the hue and cry of noticing things that make sense only in the landmark of one's sensibility in the past. The realm of the past imposes its regulatory, descriptive, prescriptive, and analytical modes. Understanding becomes bound within the sedimentation of the past making sensibility. Thus, any corner of possibility and plausibility may stay out in the geographical signification of the past oriented presence.

Things easily go unnoticed and liminal spaces become readily forgotten. Absence brings its own rationale and enunciation: it validates substantiation through validating the sensibility of the identifiers of the past.

The validity of the presence is exposed to the standards of the past. One can never experience the presence in absentia but the past oriented sovereignty of absence legitimizes the meaning of being only through the channel of connecting to the past.

So this might be analogically similar to one's having a tea in the present moment while being completely away from the experiential connection of having the tea.

The more absence goes away; the more authenticity evaporates.

This evaporation may unfold its impact in searching for the endorsement within the templates of the other in a psychoanalytical context.

The presence is the emancipative element in returning one into his/her wholeness and well-being.

The fragmentation of one's being in a collectively sporadic subjective engagement may impose a pretentious belonging to the personas of one's beings.

This would downgrade the possibility of experiencing the genuine connection to one's feelings, wants, desires, needs, aspiration, and objectives. Instead, one becomes obsessively preoccupied with seeking confirmatory responses on behalf of the *Other* and its fragmented manifestations in validating the subject matters of attention.

In absence, the attention is there but not being there: it travels through the meanders of multifarious cognitive, emotional, and behavioral prompts that have strengthened their force with the gap between the presence and the experience.

The combinatory mechanisms of the previously established perceptual, emotional, cognitive, and behavioral components of one's indulgence in the fragmented beings would minimize and weaken the possibility of celebrating here and now.

This resonates with creating a logic of possibility that translates relationship only through a previously established and validated parlance of top down hierarchical conceptualizations. It, therefore, does not leave much room for connecting the disconnected since the connection needs to be stably connected through a familiar analytical connection.

With absence, creativity dissipates. Absence teaches the formula of familiarity in the school of the known whereas presence highlights the attention towards the unknown.

The phenomenology of absence triggers decontextualized connection where signifiers and signified are embedded within an interpretive discursive discourse of signification with their attention towards the past.

Presence and absence may mostly demonstrate their sensibility when one loses some one and becomes deprived of feeling his/her presence. In another level, presence may be well applied to cognitive, emotional, and behavioral dimensions where one may display his/her emotional availability and his/her cognitive accessibility thus bringing about attunement and inter-subjectivity.

In the meantime, disciplinary scholarship may also be embedded in presence or absence. Presence warns against an absence based psychology where infatuation with methods and preoccupations with standardization would give rise to a decontextualized psychology.

Our world is embroiled in absence and fragmentation. Acceleration, accumulation of tasks, and massiveness of chores and routinized activities escalate the intensity of absence and decrease the presence and its experiential implications.

This book explicates the underlying phenomenological components of presence in its broadest realm and focuses on its consequential fruition namely mindfulness. The chapters warn against an absence based psychology where infatuation with methods and preoccupations with standardization would give rise to a decontextualized psychology.

In the meantime, the book propounds that a presence-based psychology focuses on diverse modes of presence and facilitates the process of embracing a comprehensively experiential presence.

Each chapter delineates the interconnected relationship of presence and proactivity in a wide variety of psychological contexts and their implications for developing further elaborate modes of possibilities.

The discussions may ultimately lead to the emergent mindfulness in the process of presence seeking moments of reflexivity where the performative sense of observation would intermingle with the narrative mode of description.

To enhance the levels of presence through mindfulness is argued to be at the centerpiece of a fairly comprehensive connection to one's being. The book argues how this enhancement may facilitate the process of becoming more proactive in the dialectics of being and becoming.

Mindfulness would entail an intentional presence where one chooses to bring his/her attention to the present moment while meticulously and openly looking for novel things at the moment. This would require a deliberate preparation to look at alternative perspectives which unfold themselves in the process of living in the moment.

I

THE PHENOMENOLOGICAL PSYCHOLOGY OF MINDFULNESS

Mindful Ways of Experiencing

In the midst of the hectic controversy over the analytical account of the mind and behavior and its diverse modalities which was characterized in "hot approach vs. cold approach" (see, for instance, Zajonc, 1984; De Jaegher et al., 2010), it was Ellen J. Langer who changed the question of how people think into do people think at all?

The hot perspective which goes back to 1950s and 1960s was merely interested in the unconscious elements that produced certain types of performance. Thus, any performance, based on the hot perspective, was ultimately embedded within the unconscious interactive process with idiosyncratic emotional, cognitive, and behaviors categories. It was the realization of the hidden, clandestine, cryptic, and latently unconscious elements that contributed to the configuration of specific behavioral manifestation (see, for instance, Zajonc, 1984).

An alternative perspective known as the cold approach was inspired by computer-oriented discoveries and focused on the cognitive interplay of the influencing factors of a performance. The focus from the impulsive and unconscious sedimentation of a behavior was here replaced with an interest on the analytical, computational, and serial processing of information and their implications for decision making in a performance.

A search for the computational analysis of the performance and its original elements was encouraged in the cold perspective with the intention of identifying the systematic generative constituents of a performance (see, for instance, De Jaegher et al., 2010; Rendel et al., 2011).

Both perspectives were challenged by critical approaches that indicated how each of the hot and cold outlooks overlooked some of the significant influential factors of a performance. The result was the combination of both perspectives into what was later called the warm look (see, for instance, Sorrentino, 2003; Sorrentino and Higgins, 1986).

Dual process theories of social cognition examined two types of information processing which considered both hot and cold perspectives. One led to effortful and reflective type of thinking and the other one studied an automatic form of thinking with each of their implications for behavior and performance (Kruglanski and Orehek, 2007; Petty, 2004).

This was the beginning of a new horizon of scholarly conversations on the nature of awareness, the level of awareness, the content of awareness, and the manifestation of awareness. Through tens of empirically supported experiments, Langer examined the possibility of sundry modes of awareness in both inner and interpersonal relationships.

Her long-standing experiments highlighted the role of physical presence and psychological absence. In psychological absence, people are physically there but not psychologically available. Or they can be partially available.

In delineating the psychological absence, she demonstrated factors that can give rise to a decrease of presence: repetition, acting from a single perspective, premature cognitive commitment, a mere focus on the outcome and not the process, labeling, categorizations, lack of flexibility and stress, were among some of the most important contributors of mindlessness.

Langer's experiments corroborated that deep down psychological and even physical mishaps, there lies the sovereignty of mindlessness where people fail to welcome new information, fail to be sensitive toward context, cannot celebrate the possibility of multiple perspectives, get stuck in one perspective, cannot go beyond regulations and consider rules as unquestionable.

The absence-oriented state of mind or mindlessness was also characterized by a tendency where the past over-determined the present to the effect that people were subjugated by the tyrannical subjugation of the pre-conceived schemas, regulations, and categories.

Langer's main theme of mindfulness propounded that the foundational component of mindfulness begins with a deliberate attempt to look for novelty, seek newness, search for freshness, and pay attention to the unfamiliar.

This may be opposite to what the mainstream attitudes and pedagogical and educational systems have already prescribed namely live through the habits, take for granted what is already known, move from the position of knowing and abide by a logical and linear connectedness. Mindfulness revamps the taken for granted paradigms of habituation, socialization, cultivation, and assimilation and argues that there are plenty but infinite possibilities of explorations that may be easily overlooked, neglected, ignored, and marginalized through maximizing one paradigm of possibility.

People to whom mindfulness is only synonymous with meditation based on the works of John Kabat-Zinn (2003, 2005), may find it interesting to know that Langerian mindfulness suggests that although meditation can facilitate the process of mindfulness implementation, yet one can achieve mindfulness without meditation too. The core constituent of the latter transpires through a deliberate, intentional, open, and curious attention toward the novel manifestations of the unfamiliar.

Langer argues that we are so compressed by virtue of our familiar modes of beings that we hardly question them and we rarely ask for multiple new alternatives that lie by the same familiar.

Highlighting the impact of mindless and its features, Langer (2009) writes:

> When we learn mindlessly, we look at experience and impose a contingent relationship between two things—what we or someone else did and what we think happened as a result. We interpret that experience from a single perspective, oblivious to the other ways it can be seen. Mindful learning looks at experience and understands that it can be seen in countless ways, that new information is always available, and that more than one perspective is both possible and extremely valuable. It's an approach that leads us to be careful about what we "know" to be true and how we learn it. At the level of the particular experience, each event is unique. (pp. 29–30)

Langer (2009, 2005, 1997, 1985, 1987) indicates that mindfulness "leads us to greater sensitivity to context and perspective, and ultimately to greater control over our lives." Langer (2000) considers mindfulness as something that liberates us from our limitations and allows us to learn as creatively and openly as possible. On the other hand, she indicates that mindlessness is not only an impediment for novel ideas and distinctions but is also imposing mind-sets "that have been mindlessly accepted to be true."

MINDFULNESS AND PRESENCE

Our habituated ways of knowing may strongly keep us in a process where the emotional, cognitive, and behavioral mechanisms from the past over-determine the present moment and therefore our experience of the moment is victimized through the flux of the past combinatory elements. This may have different implications for limiting, distorting, containing, incarcerating, and constricting our present experience to the effect that the experiential process may be detached from the nature of the present experience. Instead of experiencing the taste of an apple in the immediate now and the moment, for instance, the taste might remind us of a previously experienced flavor or it might give the recollection of our grandparents' garden of apples. In any case, we become devoid of the present moment.

Langerian mindfulness argues for a state of mind that can get fully connected to the moment while remaining flexibly open to explore the flow of the moment and its multiple possibilities. This is the vital ingredient of Langerian mindfulness which generates a genuine sense of presence. Presence entails a mental, cognitive, emotional, behavioral, and an overall existential preparation to examine and get engaged in the immediate now. In this sense, Langerian mindfulness is not merely about cognition but is an ontological shift where one may experience the radical transformation of consciousness.

This involves a shift of attention in a choice-oriented mode that is to choose to manage the attention. Choice is the key ingredient of mindfulness: with an enhancement of mindfulness, one learns to see the implementation of choice and the power of selective attentiveness. In an absent-oriented mode or mindlessness, attention is scattered and sporadic.

Langerian mindfulness offers a special tilt in the experiential and phenomenological process of connectedness to the present moment.

The presence is of great significance here as it provides the essence of "being there." The athlete who is being there experiences the unifying theme of presence away from multiplicity, absence, and sporadic cognitive and emotional engagements.

Langer's revolutionary concept of mindfulness demonstrates that presence is mostly concealed to oblivion through mindless multitasking, incarceration within one perspective, inflexibility in revising one's position of being, and lack of authenticity in the moment to moment experiential presentation of self.

When mindlessness is rampant, one lives and acts in absentia: he/she is all over the place; he/she fails to experience the panacea of lively connectedness to the present moment as the occupation of the past or the future would prevent one from an active lingering in the moment. Mindfulness blooms in presence and through presence. It unifies the aptitudes, abilities, competencies, and skills into one and allows the person to experience the wholeness of himself/herself in the interconnectedness of action and the agent. The subjective experience and the objective experience intermingle with one another and the dichotomy of the subject-object relationship ceases to operate. The wholeness within the experiential process of mindfulness is intertwined with the consequential ontological transformation of consciousness where being and mindfulness consummate together.

In absence, multiplicities grow in that the focus is gone and the perspective management ceases to operate. With the rise of multiplicities, one may experience fragmentation where fullness of attention goes away and presence is replaced by absence. Absence is degenerating wholeness and brings about division. You may be physically there but not psychologically there or you may be cognitively there but not emotionally there.

The goal of mindfulness is to create and promote a whole oriented presence where the full-fledged presence may open up to viewing multiple possibilities. When in mindfulness, one may enjoy the benefit of connectedness to the immediate now. The pre-conceived mindset of possibility may keep the sensibility of possibility within pre-determined mapping of possibility and thus limits the meaningfulness of possibility based on the paradigmatic analysis of the previously established categories. If you had gone to people a hundred years ago and discussed with them the possibility of making an I-Phone in the present format, people would have described it, perhaps with derision, as impossible.

This may transpire in a group of athletes through a promotional prompt of communication where everyone is asked to disengage from the scattered shower of multiplicities and massiveness of mental preoccupations. The tale of the Oxford rowing crew's 1987 race against Cambridge may elucidate the vitality of such moments (Topolski, 1989).

> After losing the race in 1986, the Oxford boat club faced a long year before meeting Cambridge again. Aside from the wounded pride and standard training, those 12 months included an inordinate amount of drama. One of the 1986 Oxford crew members, an American named Chris Clarke, returned the following year with several experienced American rowers who had enrolled in Oxford. Their plan was, simply, to put out as strong team as they could, one that could not possibly lose to Cambridge again.
>
> As often happens in sports, things did not go as planned. The team had little camaraderie, and members even showed outright hostility toward each other and the leaders of the club. The newer rowers did not agree with the established training routines; they felt that the training routines were not necessary to ensure success. Disagreements over training methods resulted in an attempt to oust the club president (who also rowed on the team). When this revolt failed, half of the team members, led by the American contingent, quit the club with just 6 weeks to go before the boat race.
>
> A poorly trained, substandard crew was left to prepare for the race. The team showed no unity, had little confidence in leaders, and was largely disinterested in the race. Training runs and exhibition competitions resulted in poor times, further decreasing team confidence. Team members admitted to each other that they had little chance of winning the race and provided a wide variety of reasons for this impending failure.
>
> However, the team did not fail. Instead, it pulled off a historic upset victory against Cambridge. From a social psychological perspective, one key aspect of this triumph was that, during a final team retreat, the team voted on the lineup for the race with Cambridge, inserting the maligned club president into a key position in the boat.

> From that point onward, although time was running out, the crew's training performances were excellent (Topolski, cited in Schneider et al., 2012).

This may be further studied in view of the prompt mode of the communication where one may see the attempt of the coach to disengage the crew from mindless entrapment. Addressing the team, the coach said: "This is your weather," I told the crew, and "out there it's your water, no one can cope with those waves like you guys can, at least of all Cambridge. You have the weight and technique for rough water—and better still, you have the nerve for it. And, I don't think Cambridge has that nerve. If it stays like this, I really think you could pull it off tomorrow" (pp. 274–75 cited in Schneider et al., 2012).

The above-mentioned story may explicate the importance of influencing one's performance through developing a sense of connectedness to the significance of the present moment and its potential resources. This may be facilitated through a motivational speech as was done in this case. On an individual level too, one may leap beyond the mindlessly accepted self-talk of negativity and helplessness and engage in productive proactive and positive self-talk.

Langerian mindfulness propounds that thoughts can be taken as a series of choices and choices are ultimately changeable. The sovereignty of the recursive parade of mindlessly accepted thoughts would impose an unquestionable and indubitable obedience to them.

So one can't forbear paying attention to them, and right after the attention, the endorsement happens.

According to Langerian mindfulness, paying attention to a thought is a choice. One can always choose not to choose this choice. Furthermore, one may choose to attend to the thought but chooses not to endorse the thought. With an increase of mindfulness and its components including noticing new things and increasing the experiential and phenomenological presence in the moment, one would be able to ascertain and acknowledge the power of agency namely the power of his/her choices over the context.

Mindlessness suggests the availability of no power and no agency. It is equipped with the automatic regurgitation of loss of power and is devoid of agency. Mindless driven performance is entrenched within the habitual powerlessness of the tyranny of the past so in Langerian doctrine the past over-determines the present and there is no presence except the precipitating effects of the past stricken presence.

In the tale of the Oxford rowing crew's 1987 race against Cambridge, the coach wages his endeavor to bring the focus of the team to the present moment. He then inspires them with the power of choices and hopefulness. Langer's experiments have indicated that with an increase of mindfulness, one would be able to have more influence to empower others. It is interesting to know that mindfulness opens up the way for activating moments of connectedness to both the inner and the external world. On the other hand, social psychologists and researchers who have studied performance indicate that positive messages, an enhancement of conversations among team members between and during plays, expression of emotions and team cohesion are positively correlated with positive performance (see Dale and Wrisberg, 1996; Lausic, et al., 2009; Widmeyer and Williams, 1991; DiBerardinis et al., 1983; Sullivan, 1995; Sullivan and Feltz, 2003).

Langerian mindfulness highlights the psychological ontology of "being there" as an essential element of a peak performance. The corollary of the psychological ontology purports a perceptive and sagacious distancing from the familiar avenues of being with a search for the unfamiliar.

Thus, mindfulness ends up being about the being itself and not cognition or emotion. When performance and being are mutually tied to the fountains of wholeness in the moment, the performance would intrinsically move in the heart of expansive mindfulness. In other words, mindfulness expands ontologically and experientially and with the expansion of each moment where the performer experiences the fullness of the link to the presence, his/her performance increases. It is like walking over a mountain where each step allows you to be more in touch with new horizons of possibilities.

According to Langerian mindfulness, these horizons are sequentially and simultaneously giving rise to different stages of mindfulness to the effect that each stage is enriching the scope and breadth of the previous stage and hence liminal spaces are discovered through the expansion of the creative moments. Liminal spaces are spaces unknown to the mindlessly calculated parameters; they are unbeknownst to the logical driven mentality. Yet, they unfold themselves as the process of present oriented vivacity increases. In doing so, outcome goals, process goals, and performance goals are united in the interactive process of mindfulness and living in the moment.

2

CREATING MINDFUL POSSIBILITIES

The psychology of possibility is one of the conspicuous landmarks of the shift in Langerian mindfulness. The psychology of possibility offers a shift from "knowing what is" to "knowing what can be" (Langer, 2009, p. 15).

The psychology of possibility critically questions the sovereignty and subjugation of knowing; it strikingly shatters the reliance on the structural repose of habitual ways of thinking; it ruptures the dependency on the plethora of circumscribing factors including our thoughts, our experiences, our schemas, and our assimilating concepts. The psychology of possibility harbors the flight from the routinized discourse of entanglement within the prescribed signifiers to the infinite realm of becoming. The psychology of possibility is not a positivist-driven psychology with a concentration on logical positivism, linear modes of thinking, and illness models. The psychology of mindfulness is a psychology of hope, faith, and meaning making; it is a psychology of self-empowerment, self-growth, and self-consummation. The psychology of possibility does not lie in negation and disconnectedness; it is a psychology of connectedness: it illustrates the possibility of repositioning one's self through a non-evaluative process in which negativity does not stop the process of furthering one's movement.

The psychology of possibility celebrates the process of becoming through a mindful examination of choices. The psychology of possibility allows one to linger in the spaces of being and becoming. The psychology of possibility highlights how our mindsets are paralyzed within the illusion of stability; the psychology of possibility enlightens the possibility of an exquisitely fresh experience with revitalizing implications. In elucidating this, Langer (2009) indicates that "we hold things still in our minds, despite the fact that all the while they are changing. If we open up our minds, a world of possibility presents itself" (p. 18).

The psychology of possibility does not look for endorsement through probabilities; it encourages thinking beyond the stability of the established patterns of thinking. In dissociating from the dependency of mindset based on a mere focus on "is" than "can be," Langer (2009) writes:

> There are many cynics out there who are entrenched in their beliefs and hold dear their view of the world as fixed and predictable. There are also people who, while not cynical, are still mindlessly accepting of these views. A new approach to psychology and to our lives is needed because the naysayers—those who demand empirical evidence are—winning. It is they who have determined what's possible and what's achievable, to our collective detriment. (p. 18)

A Langerian understanding of psychology is constantly seeking the dialectics of construction and deconstruction where the certainty of the assumptions and the hubris of knowing can be openly exposed to the manifestation of uncertainty and a quest for alternative possibilities. A Langerian understanding of psychology offers a new reference point that goes beyond the government of numbers and the illusion of precision. This new reference point propounds that one's level of being can be continuously heightened not through a repose in the repertoire of schemas and engagement in the cognitive process of Piagian assimilation and accommodation but through a genuine and mindful exploration of the flux of novelty and its innovative unfolding as one flexibly and yet persistently embraces the incessant flow of presence. Although it can lead to an inclusion or a discovery of flow in Csikszentmihalyi's (1990) sense, this is different, since it serves as a springboard for fostering higher stages of being. In doing this, Langerian perspective offers a new paradigm.

Psychology has long been sitting on the pulpit of intercepting actualities and has thus produced the borders and the definers of the psychological products within the prescribed paradigmatic analysis of what is out there. A Langerian perspective, however, propounds a concentration on potentialities and possibilities where the innovativeness of the next moment is by no means pledged by the attractors of the sovereignty of the familiar. This moves in line with fighting for otherwise where Creativity targets the unknown, the unfamiliar, and the unexplored. It searches the mystery within mastery, the opening within the blockage, the revolution within stability, the disintegration within integration, the decomposition within the composition, the indeterminacy within determinacy, and the light within the darkness.

To understand the creation of possibilities through the act of poetry, one needs to disengage himself/herself from what Langer (1998) calls "premature cognitive commitment." A poetic based phenomenology would open up the possibilities for new modes of expressiveness since sensibility is no longer in effect through the previously made schematic analysis. This requires a preparation to be in Langerian term (1997) "mindful." This mindfulness, in Langerian terms, requires noticing new things, paying attention to a flux distinct from the past, exploring the layers of the unexpressed. The essence of Langerian mindfulness occurs in engagement.

Being engaged constitutes one of the main components of mindfulness. As people mindfully get engaged in the process of experiencing the experience, they are not only there but also *they are being there*. The engagement gives rise to living in the moment in a mindful manner. In mindless phenomenology, youths are not living in the moment. Their working memory keeps them in the established categories.

Once one is locked in an information, he/she is not looking for alternative ways of looking at the subject of the experience. This may help us understand how in a mindlessness-based phenomenology, propositions are considered absolute whereas in a mindfulness-based living experience the statements and propositions are presented in a conditional format. The conditional formatting would allow the youths to understand the tentativeness of the proposition and thus would help them to look into other possibilities.

In a revolutionary perspective on our modes of thinking and expressiveness, Langer (2009) propounds that moving from a position of not knowing would provide us with the panacea of more possibilities to express the unexpressed: it allows us to go beyond the pre-established discourses of thinking and it promotes paying attention to novel things.

Explaining this mindful phenomenology of creativity, Langer (2009) writes:

> When we learn mindlessly, we look at experience and impose a contingent relationship between two things—what we or someone else did and what we think happened as a result. We interpret that experience from a single perspective, oblivious to the other ways it can be seen. Mindful learning looks at experience and understands that it can be seen in countless ways, that new information is always available, and that more than one perspective is both possible and extremely valuable. It's an approach that leads us to be careful about what we "know" to be true and how we learn it. At the level of the particular experience, each event is unique. (pp. 29–30)

A Langerian perspective on psychology is creative and creational in that it continuously and not continually encourages innovation and novelty and induces a constant engagement with revisiting the perspective that positions the actor. This, ipso facto, brings an exquisite manifestation of the experience where the experience is not merely compartmentalized within the repetitious patterns of the priming, cultivation, or association. In delineating the function of this experience, Langer (2009) writes:

> When we learn mindlessly we look at experience and impose a contingent relationship between two things—what we or someone else did and what we think happened as a result. We interpret that experience from a single perspective oblivious to the other ways it can be seen. Mindful learning looks at experience and understands that it can be seen in countless ways, that new information is always available, and that more than one perspective is both possible and extremely valuable. It is an approach that leads us to be careful about what we "know" to be true and how we learn it. At the level of the particular experience, each event is unique. Why do we think we can learn from experience? That is, if events don't necessarily repeat themselves, what can one event teach us about a future event? (pp. 29–30)

A Langerian understanding of psychology, therefore, is not built upon a linear understanding of phenomenon and their relationship. The linear understanding allows one to search for sensibility, yet it imposes syntagmatic relations that need to be observed upon any examination. Langerian perspective on psychology challenges the Cartesian epistemology and the presumed discovery of law-like generalizations that appear as the foundation for deductive explanations and predictions. This might bring Langerian epistemology in close proximity with Heidegger (1959), where he questions Cartesian discourse and its subject–object orientation indicating that nothing new can be learned as understanding becomes tantamount to nothing but a repetition of what has already been included in the interpretive process. Heidegger (1959, pp. 157–58) elucidates that "[Man] is always thrown back on the paths that he himself has laid out: he becomes mired in his paths, caught in the beaten track, and thus caught . . . excludes himself from being. He turns round and round in own circle."

A Langerian understanding of psychology avoids such a circle and considers language as a choice; it invites mindful listening and warns against the mere presentation of a spectator, as, in the language of Heidegger (1959, p. 13), it "is in words and language that things first come into being and are." A Langerian understanding, therefore, focuses not on an already existing understanding but on making understanding possible and initiating understanding in multifarious and polysemic levels. In doing this, Langer (2009) suggests:

> Experience can be a feeble teacher. How do we learn when we think we are learning from experience? We look back at the experience—an experience that could be understood in countless ways—and impose a relationship between two things even though many other relationships could have been constructed. Once we have the relationship in mind we look for confirmations and eliminate alternative understandings. So experience too often "teaches" us what we already know. Sometimes yesterday's progress is today's failure.
>
> We try walking on a broken leg that is healing and we're doing fine, and then we see we've pushed ourselves too far and the next day we have to take it easier. We could have understood our past experiences to lead us to give up, take it easy, or try harder. (pp. 30–31)

A Langerian understanding of psychology reproaches the scientific dogmatism and its consequential reductionism and critiques the establishment of a determinate reality for human intellect. A Langerian perspective explicates the significance of understanding the process, and in doing this it brings into perspective James's (1971) view that life is so opulently rich. In doing this, Langerism is very much in common with James's notion of indeterminism and his illustration of the limitation of the knowing and the knower. Yet, along with James (1956), Langerism encourages the search for "real, genuine possibilities in the world," as it fosters and facilitates the process of transcending the ordinary to higher and mystical stages of consciousness or, in the language of James (1958), "from a less into a more." Thus, Langerism may serve as a preamble for a transcendental process of being and becoming away from the quotidian engagements that only resonate with the platitudes of the entanglement with the ordinary. In describing the possibility of such a process and its experiential understanding,

James (1971) writes:

> There are possibilities [in us] that take our breath away of another kind of happiness and power based on giving up our own will and letting something higher work for us, and these seem to show a world wider than either physics or philistine ethics can imagine. Here is a world in which all is well. (p. 266)

The point here, however, is to argue for a broader demonstration of Langerian mindfulness where, in addition to its significant applications and implications, mindfulness can be taken as a foundational perspective that can serve as a leading theory. Langerism can, then, be taken as a new reference point for psychology where the research, teaching, learning, and, more importantly, understanding can be fundamentally transformed. This transformation, besides its numerous practical benefits, can give rise to attention toward the unprivileged voices that may have been concealed to oblivion in the mindless entrapment of the discourses of power. Indicating how the mindsets on expertise would develop mindlessness, Langer (1989) explains how the hegemony of those who construct the dominant narratives in a society have the power to exclude people and groups. She elaborates the mindlessness beneath the narrative structures that turn out to be the internalized truths within a society and expounds on the society's mindlessness to abide by the standards established by the so-called experts. Langer (2009) demonstrated the impacts of the dominant discourses in suppressing marginalized voices and depicts the extension of the mindlessness to the individual level where individuals are mindlessly subscribed to the hegemony of the discourses that they search for their meaning through an automatic obedience to the norms set by the dominant discourses. As Langerism would open up numerous possibilities for exploring the significant interstices that may have been largely overlooked and their marginalizing implications, it can also be of vital importance for practitioners within the psychological field. To exemplify, some therapists may be mindlessly entrapped by the categories such as cross-generational coalitions, rigid boundaries, or self-differentiation, and accordingly may not be able to examine the dehumanizing implications of such categories. However, some therapists' mindless clinging to the scientific dogma and the persistence to reductionism may reveal the pernicious impacts and dehumanizing effects of reducing people to DSM-IV diagnoses. Langerism questions the therapists' privileged access to the truth and saliently highlights the mindful process of revisiting the assumptions and the views that, if not reexamined, can lead to insidiously paralyzing outcomes and consequences. In line with this, Langerism would facilitate the process of a genuine cultural psychology where the intercultural phenomena would be studied not on the strength of the dominant positive paradigmatic analysis but by virtue of a quest for understanding while lingering in the unfamiliar paradigm. This may also suggest that truths can be institutionalized, and the process of institutionalization of the truth may hamper the process of a recondite cultural understanding. To do this, Langerism can be of great service to psychology of mass media where the social construction of reality would unfold itself.

A SHIFT FROM EPISTEMOLOGY TO ONTOLOGY

Coming from a mindful perspective and looking for alternative ways of interpretation, one may also suggest that mindfulness is a stage of being; a higher being that is well connected to knowing: knowing becomes being. Ha'iri Yazdi (1992) explores this relationship of knowing and being in the following way:

> The inquiry into the nature of the relationship between knowledge and the knower can lead to the very foundation of human intellect where the word knowing does not mean anything other than being. In this ontological state of human consciousness the constitutive du-

> alism of the subject–object relationship is overcome and submerged into a unitary simplex of the reality of the self that is nothing other than self–object knowledge. From this unitary simplex, the nature of self-object consciousness can, in turn, be derived. (p. 1)

Langerian mindfulness, therefore, presents a shift from epistemology to ontology. It opens up a new state of being. Psychology, having gotten itself disengaged from any ontological engagements, can view mindfulness on the strength of an epistemological position. The search for mindfulness in psychology is, thus, conducted within the epistemological priming of the presentations that, according to the very nature of Langerian mindfulness, may have not been very mindful of the multiple perspectives outside the realm of the epistemological endeavors. To put it in another way, psychology's long engagements with the quest for sensibility within the familiar epistemological paradigms may have accentuated the process of an overindulgence in the epistemological positioning at the cost of an ongoing mindlessness toward the ontological engagements.

Langerian understanding of psychology develops a link between both realms, namely epistemology and ontology, and openly embraces the possibility of an ontological influence on the epistemological realm. It could, among other potential services for the world today, offer a more mindful understanding of the need for a solid interdependence between the two known realms that have mindlessly turned back at one another. A Langerian understanding of psychology, hence, opens up the possibility for a genuine interdisciplinary and multidisciplinary search with an emphasis on the distinctions of each operating perspective.

If mindfulness is taken as being, a higher stage and a state of being at that, psychology's task would find itself inextricably tied to an etiological responsibility, namely providing a great repertoire of mindfulness for fostering growth in both individual and social levels. Langerian understanding of mindfulness can, therefore, be a great tool at the service of both cultural and political psychology where the perfunctory knowing of relations and relationship can bring detrimental implications for world peace and security. Langerian understanding of psychology may accordingly promote rich opportunities for affecting the quality of life with positive social, individual, and political implications.

Langerian presentation of mindfulness, hence, brings a fundamental deconstruction of some of the mainstream psychological assumptions that have dominated our psychological understanding. Langerian mindfulness and its consequential experiments have brought new findings in numerous areas of psychological research including creativity, health, performance, education, learning, and decision-making. This, can be taken as a micromanifestation of the Langerian version of mindfulness, whereas in the macrolevel Langerian presentation of mindfulness propounds a transformative process of examination of psychological phenomena; it augurs changes in psychological thinking while going beyond the realm of thinking.

Langerian understanding of mindfulness can be interpreted as a new understanding of psychology in which the reference points for the psychological analysis would be openly exposed to a mindful excavation of both the perspective and the actor.

Langer may be described as the forerunner of the Western psychology of possibility. Contrary to the mainstream psychology that legitimizes psychology's dependency on unitary simplex of the reality of the self that is nothing other than self-object knowledge. From this unitary simplex, the nature of self-object consciousness can, in turn, be derived (p. 1).

Mindful creativity lies in a comfortable dissociation from the rigid mental structures that prescribe an obedience to what is known.

The essence of creativity and critical mindfulness begins with questioning and challenging the frameworks of perception inherited from the past. It moves beyond the ordinary and every day discourses, memory's impact, and the interference of association of ideas.

When the new horizons of thinking beam, ere the spectrum of looking into things in a novel way glow.

Creativity starts with a journey inside and outside the existing values, prevalent practices, pervasive approaches and common modes and exercises. It begins with questioning the flux of order, the arrangement of presentation, the apparition of the happenings, the manner of unfolding, the ways of showering, the moments of satisfaction, the pleasures of certainty, the avenues of solutions, the mansions of conclusiveness, the comfort of sufficiency, the impressiveness of suppositions, the forcefulness of associations, the obviousness of realization and the easiness of acceptance.

Creativity challenges the way things are and explores other ways things can be. Creativity fights for otherwise. Creativity targets the unknown, the unfamiliar and the unexplored. It searches for mystery within mastery, the opening within the closure, the possibility within actuality, the passage within the blockage, the revolution within stability, the disintegration within integration, the decomposition within the composition, the indeterminacy within determinacy, the plurivocity within univocity, the imperturbability within perturbability, and the light within the darkness. Creativity rises in the midst of habituation, acclimatization, and familiarization and seeks novelty, exquisiteness, innovation, and revivification. Creativity does not succumb to the deluge of ordinariness, commonality, platitudinous, and conventionality.

As our mindlessness increases, she argues, our creativity and the act of drawing novel distinctions decreases. It is only in mindfulness that we can look into alternative ways and notice new and novel things.

It is at the time of mindfulness that we can actively live in the present, situate ourselves in the moment and think creatively about perspectives and possibilities. On the contrary, it is in the mindlessness that we unquestionably rely on our mind-sets and ignore alternative ways.

Langer challenges many of our beliefs about learning and argues that these are some of the mind-sets that have been mindlessly learned and work to our detriment. She recommends mindful learning and propounds its consequences: "The result is that we are then able to avert the danger not yet arisen and take advantage of opportunities that may present themselves.

Langer may be described as the harbinger of the Western psychology of possibility. Contrary to the mainstream psychology that legitimizes psychology's dependency on the observer's version of understanding and their authoritative privilege in endorsing the observer-driven truth, Langerian psychology examines the hegemony of the context-oriented truth and probes the necessity for looking at the a priori assumptions that act as the driving forces of the psychological analysis. In doing this, Langerian understanding of psychology would potentially offer an in-depth look at a wide variety of psychological assumptions that are implicitly taken for granted.

Opening up the possibility in light of mindfulness may suggest the deliberate attempt to broaden the perspective. This may also require an intentional flexibility to welcome new categories, new horizons of being and becoming, novel arenas of sensibility and fresh avenues of exploration. This may be usually discouraged as entrapment by categories incarcerate the likelihood of going beyond the pre-defined borderlines of validity, sensibility, and plausibility.

Langerian mindfulness (1989) highlights the role of getting settled in the perfunctory repose of the categories and indicates that "mindlessness sets in when we rely too rigidly on categories and distinctions created in the past. . . . We build our own and our shared realities and then we become victims of them—blind to the fact that they are constructs ideas" (p. 11).

During the past thirty years, there have been more than 45,000 published articles on depression, with only 400 on joy (Hall, 1998). Psychology seems to have been largely encapsulated and entrenched within the categories created by the pervasive discourse of negativity within the bedrock of the illness model. The pervasiveness of the categorization has brought an implicitly induced mindlessness that has prevented most of the research in psychology from breaking the establishment and the tyranny of the categories. The confirmatory reference points have reclaimed their sensibility within the paradigmatic analysis of the categories, which, notwithstanding their generative power of conducting reflection on the categories, their ramifications, and their imbrications, have attested to a tacit mindlessness in which the sovereignty of the established categories has not been mindfully deconstructed.

3

PSYCHOLOGY'S CONTEXTUAL ANALYSIS

One of the main reasons of psychology's entrapment in the illness model and its emergent categories may be examined in the contextual analysis of psychology's growth and development. Both in the United States and in Western Europe, psychology has been influenced, at least as much as the products are concerned, by the underlying social, economic, political, and even military factors. The Great Depression, the World Wars, the Cold War mentality of fear and anxiety, the probability of increasingly growing forces of harm and danger are among a few of the contextual elements that have potentially contributed to the significance of a direction toward which psychology has marshaled its forces.

One may need to look at the assessment tools and their initial applications for military goals to reconnoiter how psychological tools and assessments have expedited their process of growth through a recondite emplacement within the mentality of power.

The contexts, albeit varied in terms of manifestations, have strikingly impacted psychological scholarship. Darwinian theory and its operative metaphors in ruling out the possibility of a search for genuine virtues, Hobbes' epistemology of human beings' innate badness, the Soviet Union's launching of Sputnik, the first man-made space satellite, are some of the many other examples of the contextual factors that have forcibly prescribed a direction for psychology that displays its revelatory mindlessness in probing realms and perspectives beyond the formidability of the context. It seems that psychology has been extensively subjected to its contexts' oriented propensities and has been incarcerated within the definers of the contextual constraints.

On the paralyzing impact of contexts and their dictating mindlessness, Langer (1989, 1997, 2009) illustrates how contexts can induce "premature cognitive commitment" and pinpoints that "contexts can be an influence, even when we are trying to make the most precise and specific judgments" (p. 38). In an effort to break the contexts and to promote mindfulness for revisiting what has easily been concealed to oblivion, Langer (1997) challenges the underlying contextual constriction of the notion of intelligence, its roots in the nineteenth century, and its overarching inundation in determining our thinking about its possessiveness of the truth.

Elucidating the perils of contextual subjugation and its debilitating effects, Langer (1997) indicates how implicit or explicit submissiveness within the contextual borders would deprive us from adopting a proactive posture or a creative approach. Langer's points on entrapment by categories can be very helpful in understanding how psychology's incarceration within some of the preestablished categories has imposed a one-sided direction in thinking about social phenomena. Langer's illustration of mindlessness by categories would facilitate the process of looking at the psychological trends and their social implications. Once the categories have been established, they have been operative in making judgments and making decisions. If you seem to fit the categories as they have been designed, you would be automatically subjected to the defining borders of the categories. In the realm of social services, for example, one may see how this entrapment would have led to "blaming the victims for not adjusting to degrading social conditions" (Nelson and Prilleltensky, 2005).

In further exemplification of such entrapments and their social implications, Nelson and Prilleltensky (2005) write:

> As an example, the field of psychology had created intelligence testing in the UK (Francis Galton) and France (Alfred Binet) and IQ tests were imported to and refined in the US during this period. Galton and other psychologists in the area of intelligence testing were proponents of Social Darwinism (Albee, 1996a), which took Darwin's concepts of natural selection and survival of the fittest and applied them to human beings and intelligence. IQ was viewed as an innate quality of individuals, and people with low IQ scores were

> seen as inferior and unworthy, people who should be "weeded out" of society because they weakened the genetic stock. The eugenics movement, which was prominent in the 1920s, used the philosophy of Social Darwinism to advocate for the separation of the "feeble-minded" from the rest of society into institutions, sterilization of people with low IQ, and restrictions on the immigration of people deemed to be inferior (those from eastern and southern Europe, Africa and Asia). (p. 8)

One may see further depth of such mindlessly accepted categories and their social destructive implications as Nelson and Prilleltensky (2005) highlight "chilling" quotes from Albee (1981), who presents examples with instantiation of such mindlessness:

> We face the possibility of racial admixture here that is infinitely worse than that favoured by any European country today, for we are incorporating the Negro into our racial stock while all of Europe is comparatively free from this taint . . . the decline of American intelligence will be more rapid . . . owing to the presence of the Negro (Brigham [Princeton psychologist], 1923). [Massive sterilization] is a practical, merciful and inevitable solution of the whole problem can be applied to an ever widening circle of social discards, beginning always with the criminal, the diseased, and the insane and extending gradually to types which may be called weaklings rather than defectives and perhaps ultimately to worthless race types. (Grant [New York Zoological Society], 1919; Nelson and Prilleltensky, 2005, p. 8)

PSYCHOLOGY'S DISCURSIVE METAPHORIC CONSTRICTIONS

The discourse of knowledge may also be embedded within implicit or explicit modalities of mindlessness. The position of knowing might as well block the novel search for understanding. The literature in psychology is brim with examples of mindless entrapment by labels and their metaphoric implications (see Churchland, 1987). One may need to look at the research on cognition, for instance, and find out how computers and their affiliated terms and connotations gave rise to a mindless search for explorations of one of the main subject matters in psychology, namely mind.

When computers occupy the zeitgeist of scholarly works for mind, they bring a series of morphologically based concepts that develop and promote their restrictive approach toward thinking about mind. Our computer-driven research of the mind would suggest that the computer and the mind would have the same attributes: the computer can be considered with the attributes of the mind including the memory, and the human mind has the characteristics of the computer such as data processing. Notions such as coding, decoding, message, information, input, output, processing, to name a few, would structure the path of thinking about the mind in a way that other possibilities would be marginalized or overshadowed. The diverse qualities of the phenomena may be accordingly suppressed in the huge priming of the established labels that prescribe the direction and the sensibility of taking a direction to approach the subject matter. The following statements by Nadeau (1991) may cast further light on our mindless entanglement:

> Human beings are programmed in a manner analogous to programming computers. The hardware that is our brain allows us to assimilate the software of language and this software becomes the basis for encoding all aspects of the elaborate software package of a transmitted culture. (p. 171)

The same can be said when the metaphors of biology marshal their forces in thinking about social phenomena. This has turned out to be a common practice, namely borrowing terms and labels from biology or natural sciences and applying them in social sciences.

Among some recent examples, one may refer to Wilson's (1998) book, Consilience, with a biological interpretation of culture and society based on Darwinian evolutionary theory. Getting immersed in reductionism and evolutionary notions the fittest, Wilson (1998) lays huge emphasis on the only possible way of consilience where all phenomena are "based on material processes that are ultimately reducible, however long and tortuous the sequences, to the laws of physics" (p. 297).

The created models in the heart of these metaphors would limit our thinking within the domain of the prescribed structural configuration as if there were stable qualities within the social organisms. Accordingly, our intellectual endeavors to understand the phenomena would be subscribed to a quest for stability within the form. For example, if the adaptation model stands at the apex of our thinking about social phenomena, we would automatically look for the social organism's response by focusing on the best form of adaptation. The response may be taken as an explanation of the organism's stability that would help us apprehend its progress. This entangles us on a unilateral gaze at the outcome without understanding the process in which the constantly ongoing flow of events would call for a mindful understanding of the meaning within the human interactions.

A mindless indulgence on the Darwinian biology and its attributions to human phenomena in social psychology would similarly produce labels and metaphors that block our understanding of the complex interplay of diversity and its implications for understanding the meaning created by human beings in social settings.

Once we create a compartmentalization and let it pervasively serve as a leading metaphor, we assign labels that can allocate the individuals to the groups of our compartmentalization.

If the individual fails to fall into the created categories, it would be labeled as a mismatch of the group: it does not fit our classification and can thus be labeled as the opposite of our previously constructed labels. ADHD, learning disability, general disability, and so many other socially constructed labels within our seemingly psychological analysis move in that direction.

The boundaries and limits of the frequently cited labels would induce significant consequences that impede the process of transformations as they insinuate a pseudo-emplacement of truth and its associated validity and reliability within the recursive patterns of labels' pervasiveness.

A Langerian approach displays how getting encircled by the labels hamper the possibility of a genuine look at what may lie beyond our assumptions. Langer (2009) indicates that:

> Labels lead us to go on hypothesis-confirming data searches. That is, we look for evidence to support the label. Since most information is ambiguous, the result is "seek and ye shall find." The label "patient" leads us to examine behavior and life circumstances through a problem-finding lens. The label "patient" also leads us and doctors to search for illness-related symptoms. In both cases, behavior and sensations from the norm are interpreted as unhealthy. Moreover, independent cues of health may be totally ignored. (p. 135)

On the social level, we may see labels and metaphors that suggest an unquestionably established relationship between technical progress and the progress of democracy, the increase in computer mediated world and the enhancement of health and security, the advancement of technology, and the rise in human comfort.

Social psychology's engagements with some of the created metaphors have led to the promotion of certain structural thinking about social phenomena. For example, the elaboration likelihood model presented by Petty and Cacioppo (1986a, 1986b) presented a metaphoric understanding of the persuasive process that suggests an either-or way of thinking about the persuasiveness: the central routes versus the peripheral routes. Under the conditions of high involvement, the message would be processed centrally, and accordingly the receiver of the message would be highly involved in examining the content, arguments, and ideas of the message, whereas under the conditions of low involvement, the message is processed peripherally in that the receiver of the message pays no serious and central attention to issues such as content arguments and ideas in a message; instead, the receiver, under low-involvement conditions, would pay attention to issues such as attraction, expertise, and appearance of the sender, and therefore the message is peripherally processed. In central processing of the message, ELM suggest, there would be a high active participation, whereas in peripheral processing, such an active participation decreases.

The model would structure our thinking about persuasiveness through the creation of a metaphoric label namely routes that suggest we think about the message either this way (peripherally) or the other way (centrally), and we cannot think simultaneously both ways or in ways different from the peripheral or central. A mindful exploration of the peripheral may suggest that a peripheral route is also tied to a central route in that one needs to be centrally involved to some extent to proceed with a peripheral route. If the factor that activates the peripheral route activation (e.g., the attractiveness of the sender of the message) does not require any thought or consideration, can it ever bring the suggestion that, since this speaker is so attractive, thus what he/she says is perhaps true? The peripheral route, hence, is dialectically tied to a central route, to use the language and metaphor of the model.

On another level, the implications of negative labels associated with despair, inadequacy, deficiency, and despondency in psychotherapy may be explored in the context of the underlying epistemological, ontological, and etiological psychological perspectives where the focus on negativity has dissipated any mindful endeavor for searching beyond the mindlessly planted assumptions. One may go through Freud's words to detect numerous examples of the monolithically mindless attention and its embedded insinuations. In one of his assertions, Freud (1918–1996) says: "I have found little that is 'good' about human beings on the whole. In my experience most of them are trash. . . ."

The important point to note here is that through the imposition of labels and their mindless expansion, we circumscribe thinking about the psychological phenomena and limit the production of ideas, understanding, and perspectives that go beyond the limited products. The limits, therefore, identify the psychological phenomena and make it look stable and fixed. Langerian mindfulness, however, warns against the danger of this caging by the labels and argues that within these limits, the psychological phenomena and its individual or social manifestations are open to the possibilities for change and, thereby, definition: the labels should not lead us to term them as unquestionably true.

With a focus on the practical implications of mindless entrapments by the recursive patterns of labels and their inducing assumptions, Linley and Joseph (2004) examine the relationship between the deeply embedded assumptions within any psychological practice and discuss how practitioners often mindlessly go for the implementation of the practices without mindfully excavating the recondite constituents of the implicitly established messages within their mindlessly taken-for-granted axioms. On the role of these assumptions and their implications, they write:

> Further, these assumptions are typically implicit, and therefore are often uncritically accepted by practitioners trained in a particular model and a particular way of knowing. It is precisely because these fundamental assumptions are implicit that they are so often taken for granted and unchallenged, assuming the position of the status quo. (Linley and Joseph, 2004, p. 714)

One needs to read the above-mentioned citations mindfully to realize that their words are in fact tantamount to Langerian mindfulness and its call for deconstructing the layers of the assumptions that justify one's constant positioning in a single perspective.

Langer (2009) extends this from the world of psychology to the world of medicine and challenges the consecration of the mindlessly accepted principles that seem to acknowledge the ownership of knowing and knowledge to a group:

> We would be aware that medical facts are not handed down from the heavens, but in fact are determined by people under changing, different conditions. I don't think I can say often enough that medical decisions rest on uncertainty—if there were no uncertainty, there would be no decision to be made. To reveal at least some of this uncertainty would mean that while our doctors may be knowing and caring, they cannot be all-knowing. They are subject to the same biases and value-based judgments as the rest of us. But doctors often feel they have to hide their uncertainty. (p. 136)

Maddux, Snyder, and Lopez (2004) seem to have been inspired by a mindfulness when they examine the mindless implications of psychological wellness and illness, and suggest, "We cannot conduct research on the validity of a construction of psychological wellness and illness. They are social constructions grounded in values, not science, and socially constructed concepts cannot be proven true or false" (p. 321). Langerian understanding of mindfulness would help us understand how our language demonstrates our priorities and how it shapes our living and being. If the language is mindfully chosen or changes, that would bring a transformation in one's being. Once the subscription to a language is mindfully examined, the very examination can delineate the limiting conditions of the language used, and that examination would develop mindfulness in the choices that one may have.

Exemplifying the underlying elements of the use of the words "remission" and "cure," Langer (2009) indicates how our frequent exposure to the mindlessly accepted labels, names, and words would stop us from exploring our choices. She challenges the pervasive discourse of language in psychology and medicine and explains:

> The way we use language encourages people with cancer, alcoholism or depression to consider their disorders as an intractable part of who they are. Colds and headaches, by contrast, describe how we are at a particular time, not who we are. We might be able to improve "how we are" if we make decisions about what to call our ailments based on differences from one episode to the next. (pp. 129–30)

UNEARTHING THE UNDERLYING PSYCHOLOGICAL PARADIGMS

As words and labels may lead us toward mindlessness, entrapment in paradigms and perspectives may also reinforce and reiterate different forms of mindlessness.

At the center of psychological research and studies, there lies an underlying choice of perspectives in which knowing and its modes are defined. The studies, therefore, are essentially tied to their original source in that one cannot expect to see results and findings that are not compatible with their leading perspective. For instance, a Freudian perspective cannot give rise to findings that question the fundamental assumptions of Freud's views on human nature. Similarly, a humanistic psychological perspective would espouse practices and approaches that ultimately explain their sensibility within their original source. Also, a behaviorist perspective based on Skinner's law of positive reinforcement would, inevitably, search for outcomes and consequences that follow behaviors and that subsequently lead to an increase in the frequency of those behaviors. The notions of paradigms can be explored within a perspective in that a perspective or world view can entail a series of assumptions and beliefs that tend to explain ontological and epistemological relationships: they would represent how things are, how understanding takes place, how the relationships among things are established, what knowing is all about, how we discover relationships among phenomena, etc.

Kuhn (1962) critiques the cumulative process of facts and their implications for scientific progress and questions the dependency of the scientific progress on the steady accumulation of facts indicating that the progress happens only when there is a shift in paradigm.

Paradigms, Kuhn (1962) argues, can narrow one's perspective too much and prevent scientists from observing realities that fall outside of the paradigm. As Kuhn (1962) indicated, the real breakthroughs happen during paradigm shifts, when a new way of thinking replaces an older model.

A new paradigm does not comply with the old one not only because the presuppositions have changed in the new paradigm but also because the entire scientific field and its relevant problems have been redefined in light of the new paradigm. Therefore, what may be considered a problem may no longer be a problem in view of the new paradigm, and what made sense within the old paradigm may be totally nonsensical in view of the new paradigm.

For example, Fischer (2006) argued that psychological textbooks in the 1960s and 1970s defined psychology as the science that predicted and controlled behavior, and he provides a recount of the pervasive research methods based on the domination of the paradigm and indicates that

> By now, with psychology having been established as a rigorous empirical discipline, most psychologists no longer accept the "control and predict" definition and no longer cite logical positivism and related philosophical foundations, but often do count on accepted experimental procedures and statistical analysis as adequate to continue building a body of knowledge. Psychology textbooks most often define psychology as the study of human and animal behavior. (p. xx)

New paradigms are not warmly received, as they shatter the taken-for-granted assumptions. The emergence of the new paradigms is often associated with skepticism, mistrust, and disbelief: the new paradigms are unsettling, as they perturb the long-standing mindset that has already developed familiarity, comfort, and accessibility of the truth. To exemplify, those who have been recursively and extensively exposed to the hegemony of natural science as the leading master of inquiry for social science and psychology find it ineluctably hard to receive a perspective that questions the tyranny of the rational empiricism or logical positivism namely questioning the applicability and plausibility of natural science paradigms in the realm of psychology. According to Kuhn (1962):

> The physical referents of these Einsteinian concepts [space, time, and mass] are by no means identical with those of the Newtonian concepts that bear the same name. (Newtonian mass is conserved; Einsteinian is convertible with energy. Only at low relative velocities may the two be measured in the same way, and even then they must not be conceived to be the same.) (p. 101)

Deep down a psychological perspective, one may discern an orientation that not only suggests a way of looking at the world but also highlights what is important to know. Within an August Comte's orientation, for example, one may see the emphasis on the so-called facts and causes of behavior. The assumptions within a paradigmatic analysis would espouse a set of beliefs that demonstrate how knowing is possible. Once the paradigms are recursively established, they become almost unquestionable, since they tend to show the right way of knowing, acting, and thinking. Questioning the paradigms would then require disobedience from the structurally established sovereignty of the operating set of beliefs. This would lead to exclusion from the domain of the ruling paradigm with its own practical consequences.

Describing the practical consequences of a leap beyond the established paradigms, Scileppi, Teed, and Torres (2000) indicate that

> University dissertation committees and journal editors more readily accept research supporting the dominant paradigm, and foundations and government agencies are more likely to fund such research. The general population finds the result of research favoring the dominant paradigm to be more believable. These societal effects influence students and novice researchers to choose to investigate only phenomena that are declared valid by the dominant perspective. Thus, the dominant paradigm is unfairly supported, and other views are quickly discounted. (p. 12)

One may, therefore, claim that any psychological study or perspective can reveal a bigger perspective that defines, promotes, prescribes, controls, and even proscribes practical approaches, practices, and methods.

In exploring the underlying perspective within the psychological research, the foundational and constitutional paradigm appears to be operative.

The dominant paradigm in the mainstream psychology including the experimental psychology is very much close to the assumptions of the natural sciences with the notion that through the use of the quantification and the use of statistics, one can know the real world. The discourse of the positivist psychology is built on a position of certainty that knowledge is indeed attainable through the specific methodological shields. The certainty is largely borrowed from empiricism where the ideas need to be subjected to empirical investigation before they can be called scientific.

4

LANGERIAN PSYCHOLOGY

Langer's (2009) work on mindfulness can be seen as a work that questions the pervasive paradigm within the mainstream psychology. Interesting enough, she moves in line with the paradigmatic pillars of experimental psychology and demonstrates the inadequacy of the mainstream psychology. Langer's work, similar to those in the camp of hermeneutic and social constructionist psychologists, advocates that knowledge is constructed through our actions and interactions. What gives further merit to her work in this regard is her substantiation of the insufficiency of the mainstream paradigm through the use of the exclusive language of the mainstream psychology. In other words, others who have challenged the dominant paradigm of the positivist psychology have often used a language that is already marginalized in the mainstream psychology. Langer's work abides by the positivist paradigm, yet it shows how our ideas without reflecting any objective reality are constructed to rationalize or justify different discourses of domination. Langer (2009, p. 18) dissociates from the tyranny of the paradigm and indicates that "a new approach to psychology and to our lives is needed." Langer's position of challenge begins from her research on mindfulness. Langer's (2009) mindfulness questions the reliance on positivism and technical rationality while challenging the certainty of knowing. Mindfulness, according to Langer (2009), entails an active state that is associated with creation of new knowledge, welcoming new horizons of information, noticing new things, and being open to the possibility of multiple perspectives. It is through an active state of mindfulness, Langer (2009) argues, that one would embrace the complexity, uncertainty, instability, and uniqueness of the phenomena.

Through numerous experiments, she has demonstrated how the mere reliance on positivist-oriented knowing would lead to the monopoly of the legitimacy of one way of knowing, namely the so-called rational way of knowing over numerous other ways of knowing. Langer's (2009) mindfulness advocates a tilt toward the position of not knowing, since the fixed position of positivist knowing would hamper the exploration of an expansive array of epistemologies and locks the search for knowing in a predetermined point.

The questionable knowing has its roots in positivism and enlightenment whereby rationality is defined through an access to restricted avenues of awareness mainly embodied through the linear and analytical forms of thinking. Langerian mindfulness opens up the horizon for revisiting the well-established epistemologies and argues that as much as they have contributed to expansion of our understanding, they have contained our ways of thinking. Through her research on the implications of mindlessness and mindfulness, Langer (2009) highlights the significance of the contextual components including cultural, social, economic, and political contexts, and indicates how the hegemony of positivism and its aspirations to make broad comparisons have contributed to the promotion of insensitivity toward contexts thus fostering mindlessness.

Her delineation of this mindlessness would purport how the emphasis on uniformity of positivist driven methods such as questionnaire boils down to the marginalization of the contexts. In line with Bruner's (1986) distinction between the paradigmatic mode, namely the logicoscientific mode and the narrative mode, Langer (1989) recognizes narratives and presents them as an independent mode of cognition while demonstrating psychology's incarceration within natural science (logicoscientific mode) as a form of mindlessness. Langer's work has already been inspiring in micro levels in that it has encouraged, promoted, and induced research findings and studies that demonstrate the impact and implications of mindfulness for numerous areas including health, education performance, learning, and creativity. Nonetheless, the field of psychology may prosper from a shift of paradigm through Langerian mindfulness as one may also attribute the trend of some of the already-ongoing developments in psychology to an explicit or implicit inspiration from such mindfulness. This shift is inviting, as it calls upon the exploration of a wide variety of epistemologies and even ontologies that may have been concealed to oblivion due to the hegemony of discursive manifestations of the positivist-driven paradigm.

At the center of psychological research and studies, there lies an underlying choice of perspectives in which knowing and its modes are defined. The studies, therefore, are essentially tied to their original source in that one cannot expect to see results and findings that are not compatible with their leading perspective. For instance, a Freudian perspective cannot give rise to findings that question the fundamental assumptions of Freud's views on human nature. Similarly, a humanistic psychological perspective would espouse practices and approaches that ultimately explain their sensibility within their original source. Also, a behaviorist perspective based on Skinner's law of positive reinforcement would, inevitably, search for outcomes and consequences that follow behaviors and that subsequently lead to an increase in the frequency of those behaviors.

The notions of paradigms can be explored within a perspective in that a perspective or world view can entail a series of assumptions and beliefs that tend to explain ontological and epistemological relationships: they would represent how things are, how understanding takes place, how the relationships among things are established, what knowing is all about, how we discover relationships among phenomena, etc. Kuhn (1962) critiques the cumulative process of facts and their implications for scientific progress and questions the dependency of the scientific progress on the steady accumulation of facts indicating that the progress happens only when there is a shift in paradigm. Paradigms, Kuhn (1962) argues, can narrow one's perspective too much and prevent scientists from observing realities that fall outside of the paradigm. As Kuhn (1962) indicated, the real breakthroughs happen during paradigm shifts, when a new way of thinking replaces an older model.

A new paradigm does not comply with the old one not only because the presuppositions have changed in the new paradigm but also because the entire scientific field and its relevant problems have been redefined in light of the new paradigm. Therefore, what may be considered a problem may no longer be a problem in view of the new paradigm, and what made sense within the old paradigm may be totally nonsensical in view of the new paradigm.

For example, Fischer (2006) argued that psychological textbooks in the 1960s and 1970s defined psychology as the science that predicted and controlled behavior, and he provides a recount of the pervasive research methods based on the domination of the paradigm and indicates that

> By now, with psychology having been established as a rigorous empirical discipline, most psychologists no longer accept the "control and predict" definition and no longer cite logical positivism and related philosophical foundations, but often do count on accepted experimental procedures and statistical analysis as adequate to continue building a body of knowledge. Psychology textbooks most often define psychology as the study of human and animal behavior. (p. xx)

The emergence of the new paradigms is often associated with skepticism, mistrust, and disbelief: the new paradigms are unsettling, as they perturb the long-standing mindset that has already developed familiarity, comfort, and accessibility of the truth.

To exemplify, those who have been recursively and extensively exposed to the hegemony of natural science as the leading master of inquiry for social science and psychology find it ineluctably hard to receive a perspective that questions the tyranny of the rational empiricism or logical positivism namely questioning the applicability and plausibility of natural science paradigms in the realm of psychology.

According to Kuhn (1962):

> The physical referents of these Einsteinian concepts [space, time, and mass] are by no means identical with those of the Newtonian concepts that bear the same name. (Newtonian mass is conserved; Einsteinian is convertible with energy. Only at low relative velocities may the two be measured in the same way, and even then they must not be conceived to be the same.) (p. 101)

Deep down a psychological perspective, one may discern an orientation that not only suggests a way of looking at the world but also highlights what is important to know. Within an August Comte's orientation, for example, one may see the emphasis on the so-called facts and causes of behavior.

The assumptions within a paradigmatic analysis would espouse a set of beliefs that demonstrate how knowing is possible.

Once the paradigms are recursively established, they become almost unquestionable, since they tend to show the right way of knowing, acting, and thinking. Questioning the paradigms would then require disobedience from the structurally established sovereignty of the operating set of beliefs. This would lead to exclusion from the domain of the ruling paradigm with its own practical consequences.

MINDFUL BASED CHOICES

Mindlessness is embedded within automatic behaviors that entail fixed patterns of actions. Automaticity of behaviors diminishes the possibility of having a choice or discernment of implementing control over an action. An in-depth analysis of control may suggest that control is associated with the ability to influence. Langerian mindfulness argues that the ability to influence or the ability to respond lies in the intrinsic state of inner mindfulness in that the stimulus-response model may no longer be able to explain the possibility of having an action. Mindlessness can trigger a response merely because of a stimulus. In mindfulness, however, the stimulus does not impede alternative modes of action and control since the actor does not perceive the stimulus as mindlessly controlling his or her own action.

Langerian mindfulness argues that understanding the controllability of uncontrollable stimulus is activated through a perceptive understanding of the view of the actor. If the actor's view is constricted through the mindless mindset of having no control over the stimulus, the response would merely be subsumed under the impossibility of any action except the stimulus-driven one. If the actor's mindfulness is activated, he or she goes beyond the constriction of mindlessly shaped uncontrollability to understanding the multiple possibilities of the view toward the stimulus.

Langerian mindfulness focuses on choices, the heart of mindfulness. When mindful, the actor realizes the range of choices in the sequential or parallel forms of actions. Choices give rise to controllability. Let us say that one has a high level of anxiety and is mindlessly entrapped in a sense of helplessness.

In some of the best-known psychological methods, a person is asked to make a list of anxieties and worries. The list may number twenty, thirty, or more, arrayed from the most intense levels of anxiety-inducing incidents to the least intensive items. The person is later asked to rate the level of the anxiety-inducing factors from 1 to 10, with 1 being the lowest and 10 the highest anxiety-inducing. Not all items are in the range of 10. The majority of items fall between 5 and 8. The person is then asked to find which items in the ranking are controllable and which seem to be uncontrollable.

If an item is decided to be controllable, then a reduction of anxiety seems also to be controllable. For instance, if one is anxious about being late for his work, then the control lies in leaving home earlier. This facilitates the process of reducing the effect of the anxiety-inducing factor from, let's say, 7 to 6 or 5.

If an item is seen as uncontrollable, the person is asked to consider that, although the item may seem to be uncontrollable, his or her view of the seemingly uncontrollable is controllable. In other words, the way he or she explains and interprets the seemingly uncontrollable item can be controlled.

A person may equate the uncontrollability of external intrinsic factors with the uncontrollability of his or her own mode of action until he or she actively looks into the possibility of different forms of actions through a shift in his or her perception of the event. In Langerian mindfulness, attention to variability facilitates the process of anxiety and stress management.

Attention to variability suggests that contexts are constantly created, and contexts are not the same.

If someone is suffering from asthma, she can be asked to reflect on situations that intensify her asthma: when exposed to specific people or specific circumstances, her asthma might be exacerbated. Conversely, other situations may not give rise to her asthma.

The question here is, what circumstances instigate her asthma? If she is exposed to situation A and her asthma is activated, and when she is exposed to situation B her asthma is not activated, then she is asked to avoid situation A and explore what it is about situation B that does not trigger her asthma.

Attention to variability helps one implement the power of choice-making.

If one is on the way to a very important business meeting and the car breaks down, there may be different ways of approaching this event.

The external event (i.e., the broken car) is uncontrollable. There is no control over that as a materialized event. The approach to the external event, however, can be mindless or mindful. From a mindless perspective, Langerian mindfulness argues, the person considers the uncontrollability of the event tantamount to his or her own impossibility of action: he or she has no control.

From a mindful perspective, the person looks into options in a wide variety of possibilities. There are huge practical differences of action. In the mindless scenario, the person is emotionally compelled through his or her mindlessness to be stuck in the inability of action; thus, there is no ability to respond in novel ways. In the mindful scenario, the person goes beyond this mindset and explores the possibility of implementing possible modes of controlling and influencing the situation.

Langerian mindfulness argues that, in mindless forms of induced uncontrollability, the notion of having no control comes out of the certitude of a mindset that indicates the impossibility of having control. Mindlessness operates in the heart of certainty (see Langer, 2009). When mindfulness arrives, certainty is questioned.

The mindset is put under investigation. Langerian mindfulness proposes the possibility of revisiting the paralyzing paradigm of impossibility (see Fatemi, 2014). Mindlessness is induced through the pervasiveness, repetition, and monolithic compartmentalization of conceptual and practical engagements. Mindlessness, Langer argues, gives rise to a submissive obedience to the so-called long-standing rules. The rules are embedded within the pre-established plethora of assumptions that are mostly oblivious to human functionality outside their prescriptive modes. Thus, rule-oriented modes of action allow the implementation of any influence and control as long as the control is endorsed within the paradigmatic analysis of the sets of previously defined compartmentalization.

When emotions are highly involved, the person's ability to respond in ways other than what the mindlessly established emotions suggest is null and void; thus, the person's perceived control is merely defined within the boundaries of the compelling emotions.

Langerian mindfulness encourages an active, proactive state of mind where one can search for the unnoticed complexities in the status quo. When mindless, people are oblivious to exploring anything except the already materialized appearance of the status quo.

The mere concentration of the actuality of the event is embedded within the position of knowing. When taking the position of knowing, one is mindlessly assured of one's domain and power of knowing. With a position of knowing, one does not stretch one's scope of seeing what might be out there, outside the realm of knowing. Knowing is essentially embedded within a reliance on past cognitive commitments due to repetition, pervasiveness, and maximization of one single perspective (see Langer, 1989).

In a mindless state of mind, one's knowing is circumscribed, constricted, and contained within limiting borders of possibility and therefore having an influence or control is not prescribed outside the constricting path of possibilities within the mindless context. So the person is bound by the context and is condemned through the parochialism of the context.

In a mindful state of mind, the person's reference points from which to view the status quo are explored through it but are not limited by its deterministic configuration. Mindfulness encourages a search within the inner world, with its infinite possibilities. The power to influence is therefore actively induced through the possibility of embracing expansive modes of actions.

In mindfulness, the person creates the context. In mindlessness, the person is created through the context. The subtlety of mindfulness-empowering states unfolds its power to activate a nonjudgmental, challenging, and flexible experiential and phenomenological connectedness to one's inner resources.

Reactance theory and other earlier studies, including those by Glass and Singer (1972), indicated the power of the subjective interpretation of control and its implications. If you happen to live in New York and you are told that you can't leave the Big Apple for about a year, your being banned from leaving the city immediately develops discomfort, anxiety, and inner perturbability. The ban fights the inner flow of freedom. On the other hand, you may have lived in New York City for ten years without ever voluntarily leaving it. In this situation, you might never feel any sense of discomfort, in comparison with the banning situation. Here, you are not forced to question your power of choice.

Langerian mindfulness emphasizes the awakening role of the experiential and phenomenological belief in having choices. When mindless, people abide by the automatic behaviors that they have emotionally and cognitively inherited from the past. Mindfulness facilitates the process of one's liberation from the self-defeating mindsets that control the impossibility of controllability.

The psychology of possibility within Langerian mindfulness can open up novel horizons of action. Langerian mindfulness suggests that we have far more control over our health than people now realize. Langerian mindfulness suggests that, with an increase of mindfulness, people experience higher degrees of intersubjectivity and attunement. Inter-subjectivity happens when people are simultaneously in the same cognitive mode, and attunement occurs when people are concurrently in the same emotional mode.

With an increase of mindfulness, people can embrace a mind where peace is prevalent in both cognitive and emotional as well as behavioral domains. Mindlessly driven control emanates from anxiety, whereas mindfully driven control (in a Langerian version) stems from proactivity.

Langerian mindfulness proposes that, with an increase of global mindfulness, mindlessly driven control is replaced by a proactive sense of togetherness, synergy, and sensitivity to the possibility of multiple perspectives. Mindlessly driven control engenders anxiety and instills protectiveness to defend one from the anxiety.

Mindfully driven management (and not control in its pervasive sense) promotes understanding, empathy, and openness to celebrating the sensibility and plausibility of perspectives that may not make sense in the context of controlling mindlessness.

5

MINDFULNESS AND CHOICES

In discussing the power of choices and their psychological implications, one may touch upon the role of perceived control in directing one's actions.

Perceived control has often been translated as a belief that can have significant external implications; namely, a belief that can give rise to external influential manifestations. This influence has been examined in terms of positive or negative outcomes (see Burger, 1992; Lachman, 2006; Skinner, 1995; Thompson, 1981; Thompson and Heinberg, 1999).

In line with this, studies indicate that students reporting higher levels of perceived control of their academic performance displayed less anxiety, stress, boredom, and depression and gave rise to better grades than those with less perceived control (Perry, 2003; Perry et al. , 2001; Ruthig et al., 2009). Perceived control has also sometimes been studied with a focus on healthcare processes (e.g., Smith et al., 1984) or health behaviors or outcomes (e.g., Wallston and Wallston, 1981, 1982, 1984).

For example, victims of rape with perceived control over the outcomes in their lives reported less depression with fewer symptoms of post-traumatic stress six months or more after the event (Regehr, Cadell, and Jansen, 1999). Others have focused on perceived control and its clinical psychological implications (e.g., Kanfer, 1970; Rehm, 1977). People with a high degree of perceived control are able to challenge their automatic self-talk and choose proactive and positive self-talk. With an increase of perceived control, people learn how to create a new style of living, how to increase their choices, and how to come up with creative instead of automatic responses.

Some researchers on perceived control have conducted their inquiry within a correlational design, whereas others have focused on an experimental design. The former has not substantiated causal relationships with perceived control, whereas the latter has corroborated the possibility of a cause-and-effect relationship between control and the produced effect. Other studies have found the presence of some third variable in contributing to feeling of control and good health (Johnson and Krueger, 2005).

The confounding variables operating here may include ecological, environmental, familial, and external factors that may facilitate the process of attaining a feeling of control. For instance, people who are exposed to social support are able to deal with calamity and adversity in a more effective manner.

Perceived control suggests the possibility of the ability to influence one's psychological state, one's behavior, one's environment, and the outcomes and/or processes of some object of control. Loss of control is often associated with depression, anxiety, and death. There are some research findings that demonstrate an almost cause-and-effect relationship between perceived control and physical and emotional well-being. Elderly people with a belief in their good health were more likely to display perceived control over their lives; they reported more controlling approaches in their lives in general (Menec, Chipperfield, and Perry, 1999). A very early field experiment in examining the relationship between perceived control and well-being goes back to 1976, in a nursing home in Connecticut. Those residents who displayed significant signs of disengagement from life and experienced the abyss of depression and helplessness received a message that made not only a big difference in their lives but also a message that opened a new horizon on what was later known as mindfulness. Langer and Rodin (1976) instructed the director of a nursing home to convey a radically transformative message to its residents. Instead of focusing on what they could not do and what they were deprived of, the residents were encouraged to think about what they were able to do.

Langer and Rodin selected two groups: an experimental group and a comparison group. For the experimental group, the residents were exposed to messages that underscored their power of control, their ability to do things, and their sense of empowerment. Their scope of power was highlighted, and they were invited to undertake action within the sphere of their delineated possibilities: their responsibilities and their accountability were accented.

Addressing the experimental group of residents, the director conveyed the following message:

> Take a minute to think of the decisions you can and should be making. For example, you have the responsibility of caring for yourselves, of deciding whether or not you want to make this a home you can be proud of and happy in. You should be deciding how you want your rooms to be arranged—whether you want it to be as it is or whether you want the staff to help you rearrange the furniture. You should be deciding how you want to spend your time . . . if you are unsatisfied with anything here, you have the influence to change it. . . . These are just a few of the things you could and should be deciding and thinking about now and from time to time every day. (Langer and Rodin, 1976)

The control-inducing factors were explicated by the director, then he reiterated that there would be a movie shown the following week on two different nights and that the residents should decide on which night they want to attend. He also provided opportunities for each resident to select a plant and indicated that the responsibility of taking care of the plant was theirs.

For the comparison group, the director presented a different scenario. He delivered a similarly structured message to the comparison group but did not make any reference to their power of control, their ability to make a decision, or their responsibility. Although informing the residents of the movie to be shown the following week, he did not give the residents an ability to choose the night on which to watch the movie. Instead, he mentioned that they would be assigned a night on which to watch the movie. As for the plants, he gave all the residents a plant as a gift but told them that the nurses would take care of the plants.

Residents in the induced-control group displayed signs of higher happiness and higher activity in comparison with the control group. The intervention for the experimental group also made a surprising difference: it had a striking effect on the residents' health, and it tended to influence their mortality. In a second study, Rodin and Langer (1977) found that the group exposed to the empowering message lived eighteen months longer than those who did not receive the message: 30% of residents in the comparison condition died, whereas the death rate was only 15% in the experimental group (Rodin and Langer, 1977).

Shortly after Langer and Rodin's experiment, a similar study was conducted in North Carolina. Richard Schulz (1976) designed an experiment for a nursing home involving undergraduate students who visited its residents. The residents randomly assigned to the experimental group were instructed to decide when and how long they wanted to visit with the students. Residents assigned to the comparison group were not given any choice; in contrast with the experimental group, the students decided the time and frequency of the visits. Assessment of the outcome of these experiences showed that the experimental group displayed signs of higher happiness and higher activity and that they turned out to be healthier and did not take as much medication as the comparison group.

Like Langer and Rodin, Schulz was also interested in assessing the range and scope of his intervention over a longer period of time, so he revisited the nursing home twenty-four, thirty, and forty-two months after his initial intervention to inquire about the status of the participants' mortality rates. Shockingly, the experimental group in Schulz's design turned out to be in worse health and demonstrated signs of heath deterioration. Their mortality rate was higher than the comparison group (Schulz and Hanusa, 1978).

The difference in the results may be of great significance in understanding the underpinning constituents of perceived control in both experiments. In Langer and Rodin's study, residents in the experimental group experienced an enduring and sustainable sense of control, whereas in the Schulz's induced-control group, the residents experience a transient, ephemeral sense of control that ceased to operate after the students stopped visiting their assigned residents.

On one level, perceived control may be examined in the framework of attribution theory (Harvey and Weary, 1984; Kelley and Michela, 1980) or social learning theory (Bandura, 1977a; Bandura, 1977b; Rotter, 1954). The first focuses on events in the past and the analytical aspects of their experiences, and the second targets their expectancies and the future. Along with examining future- and past-related perceived control, self-efficacy and locus of control have also been employed to assess the relationship between perceived control and outcomes.

On another level, perceived control research and theory may open up a new horizon on the existential and phenomenological understanding of control. A wide variety of studies demonstrate that there are significant physiological, behavioral cognitive, and emotional changes attributable to the presence or lack of control.

CHOICE MAKING AND ITS PHENOMENOLOGICAL IMPLICATIONS

The phenomenological aspect of control may explain why and how Langer and Rodin's induced-control group, who received a message based on an enduring sense of control, acted differently than the Schulz's group, for whom the sense of control was temporary. Phenomenology discusses lived experience and its psychological implications. In a phenomenological analysis of an experience, we need to examine the subjective world of the actor and scrutinize how the subjective world is interpreted through experiences. Here, language is of great significance. We experience our experiences and we put our experiences into language. Understanding an experience provides a level of understanding that is distinct from the level of knowing. Understanding an experience is linked to the ontological psychology of the experience, whereas knowing about an experience occurs at an epistemological level. Knowing about choices is a far cry from understanding choices in the process of an action. Choice-making is the exercise of control. To acknowledge control suggests the acknowledgment of having choices. If control is perceived to be dependent on a non-sustainable source, the phenomenological experience of control ultimately stands in contrast with the implication of control. Taking away control would impose detrimental and harmful consequences (Rodin, 1986).

Langer's further studies on control provided a relationship between perceived control and the exploration of possibilities (2005, 2009). A phenomenological analysis of perceived control may underpin the process of Langer's further research on mindfulness and its implications for perceived control. Langer focuses on mindfulness as the key to having choices. She defines mindfulness as "a flexible state of mind in which we are actively engaged in the present, noticing new things and sensitive to context" (2000, p. 220).

A note of caution needs to be made here in distinguishing between two major perspectives on mindfulness. One is associated with Eastern philosophy and Buddhism, where meditation appears to be the main tool of mindfulness. The work by Kabat-Zinn moves in line with this perspective (see Kabat-Zinn, 1994). The other version of mindfulness, known as Langerian mindfulness, is associated with an experimental psychological approach with a continuous focus on creating and restructuring mindsets and perspectives along with flexibility, openness, and a proactive phenomenological presence in the moment.

Discussing the distinction between these two versions of mindfulness, Crum and Lyddy (2014) indicate that "Eastern mindfulness shines a clear light of unbiased and unattached awareness on existing mindsets whereas Langerian mindfulness involves a continual process or restructuring and creating mindsets anew" (p. 954).

Mindfulness begins with an active state of mind. In experiencing mindfulness, our passive, reactive, and automatic state of mind changes into an active and proactive state. This state is characterized through noticing new things, exploring novelty, and looking at the unfamiliar. It is creational. We create while we are mindful. In addition, mindfulness fosters an awareness of the context. As mindfulness expands, we become more sensitive of context. The past does not over-determine the present.

We pay attention to the rules, but we are not governed by them. The rules can be guiding but are not paralyzing. Mindfulness activates the experiential and phenomenological connectedness to the present moment. When mindful, we live in the moment: we experience a full engagement in the moment. Our presence is consummated through mindfulness (Langer, 2005, 2009).

Mindfulness has an influence on one's way of being, one's existential and ontological mode (Langer, 2000, 2005). Mindfulness provides the possibility of bridging the gap between the inner and outer worlds, where one ascertains the possibility of influencing both realms.

Langerian mindfulness as an approach proposes that control goes away when one is mindlessly disconnected from him- or herself. When mindless, one is constricted in an inflexible state of mind where one is steeped in an emotional, cognitive, and behavioral paralysis. This paralysis limits the power of control and imposes helplessness and desperation as the only functional parameters of being.

Mindfulness entails an experiential acknowledgment of one's empowerment in the creative process of reshaping one's cognitive, emotional, and behavioral options. It is tied to the phenomenological engagement of understanding possibilities beyond the pre-established patterns of identification.

Langerian mindfulness argues that, as soon as one is able to notice novelty in his or her status quo, he or she will be able to discern the possibility of disengagement from the status quo. For instance, if a person is solely defined in his professional role as a Chairperson and is so fully immersed in his being nothing but a Chair, this definition will impose an entrenchment of being nothing except a Chair. If the Chairship is taken away for any reason, the person perceives himself as doomed to failure since the source of his self-definition has been degraded.

MINDFULNESS BASED AGENCY

The foundational experiments of Langer and Rodin and the contrast analysis found in the studies of Schulz demonstrate a number of substantive points within Langerian mindfulness:

Langerian mindfulness focuses on agency as the main component of mindfulness in that the actor relies on his or her own agency as the initiator of the action; thus, the initiation takes place from an inward source. In Langer and Rodin's study, the residents in the nursing home realized that the action was theirs and that they needed to take it upon themselves to proceed with that. In Schulz's experiment, the residents were exposed to the contingency of agency: they were dependent on the initiation of action from outside, from the student aides who determined the timing of their social interactions. The residents had to wait for external factors to manifest themselves in the body of agency.

Langerian mindfulness with a focus on agency highlights the possibility of the implementation of agency through expanding the horizons of action: the actor discerns that the mindset of impossibility lies as one perspective out of many; a change of perspective opens up the possibility of exploring possible alternative modes of action. The change happens through activating one's power of agency to explore new horizons of possibility. The actor does not succumb to the fixation of the apparent impossibility. The residents in the nursing home in Langer and Rodin's experiment came to realize that mindset can be changed. The mindset of hopelessness and helplessness was simply a choice, and they could experience a shift of mindset through celebrating multiple perspectives. The possibility of the shift was induced through underscoring the significance of a change from the perspective of passivity to the perspective of responsibility. The ability to respond through one's own agency stood at the top of the initiation. In Schulz's experiment, the residents experienced the possibility of change through the action of others, so the agency was other-oriented: it was dependent on the initiation of others' agency.

As much as an in-depth excavation of the multifarious layers of a performance may allow us to detect and acknowledge the interconnectedness of an array of possible variables in shaping the specificity of a performance, one may set out to delve into the implications of agency as the creative force of the performer in giving rise to his/her performance. This may apply to different forms of dual process theories including the computer model of serial information processing and the neural network model of parallel information processing.

The former assumes that only one form of thinking can occur at a certain time so they rule out the possibility of a simultaneous form of both effortful and effortless thinking whereas the latter claims the possibility of simultaneousness of two types of parallel thinking (see Kahneman and Frederick, 2002).

In other words, we may let our analysis concentrate on the status of the performing agent in producing the outcome namely the performance within a specific domain. This will be ineluctably tied to a perceptive attention to both the process and the outcome as they are mutually linked to the etiological configuration of agency as the cause behind the performance.

A rigorous scrutiny of the psychological status of agency may help us notice how agency unfolds itself in the production of a special form of performance.

As we reflect on the role of agency in structuring and shaping the quiddity of a performance, we may ponder the significance of such questions:

Is the agency fully functioning as it facilitates the process of an emerging performance: is an agent behind the power of agency quintessentially connected to the creative process of a performance or is he/she half engaged in producing his/her performance? How can the power of agency enhance the efficacy of a performance? Are there ways to help an actor behind an agency to increase his/her power of agency?

Such questions would serve as a preamble to lead us toward understanding the significance of mindfulness and its implications for decision making and performance.

Langerian mindfulness gives rise to proactivity in decision making through initiating inner agency. The residents in Langer and Rodin's experiment experienced empowerment through their own novel power of decision-making, which substantiated the sustainability of the power due to its own operative functionality. The residents experienced an enduring sense of control. In Schulz's experiment, however, the residents came to see their empowerment as being at the mercy of an unenduring external and ephemeral factor.

Langerian mindfulness elaborates on the relationship between "ought" and "is" in the psychological proposition of discernment of control. The proposition declaring the possibility of ability and the practicality of change engages the propensity for initiating the action. The declarative statement of "is" in a mindful state of being, Langerian mindfulness argues, broadens the perspective of a search within sundry existential modes of being. The expansive acknowledgment of multiple perspectives elucidates the intrinsic possibility of existential choices. The declarative "is" thus carries a functional "ought" within its range of creative possibility (see, for example, Langer, 2009, 2005).

6

MINDFUL PERFORMANCE

With the increase of the power of mindfulness-based choices, one's performance may increase. In their work with Division I rowers preparing for the Olympics, Kabat-Zinn and colleagues (Kabat-Zinn, Beall, and Rippe, 1985, April) developed a mindfulness meditation program. Based on his Mindfulness-based Stress Reduction (MBSR) work, the mindfulness meditation program ranged from two weeks to seven months. During this program, the athletes sat in formal meditation individually and with their team. Self-reported benefits included: greater relaxation, increased concentration, as well as reduced fatigue and fewer negative thoughts. Furthermore, the Olympic medalists claimed that the program improved their performance (Kabat-Zinn et al., 1985, April).

Mindfulness-Acceptance-Commitment (MAC) theory of performance enhancement in the body of the Buddhist philosophy also focuses on enhancing athletic performance through mindfulness. It consists of structured session and interventions that teach athletes to be mindful (Gardner and Moore, 2004, 2006, 2007).

In the meantime, Langerian mindfulness has provided plenty of empirically and experimentally based examples where mindfulness can give rise to an enhancement of creative performance (see for instance, Langer, 2009, 2005, 1997, 1985, 1987).

As one becomes proactively involved in the creation of his/her work, he/she notices new things. This search for novelty which is of particular interest in Langerian mindfulness posits that knowledge is existentially transformed simultaneous with the radical transformation of the knower being the performer here too. Knowing and being move not only in parallel mode in Langerian mindfulness but they also become one: knowing is being and being is knowing. Nonetheless, knowing is not bound by the stability of the previously established frame of reference. In Langerian mindfulness, the intention facilitates the process of focusing on the moment to moment response style as it moves in accordance with the foundational component of mindfulness: a search for new perspective.

The mindful-based performance is intertwined with fervor and passion on the emotional side and broadening the perspective on the cognitive side. Recent year's findings of neuroscience demonstrate that our modes of thinking, our forms of actions and our objects of our attention may change the structure and function of our brains. In Langerian mindfulness, the performer is taught to train his/her attention in view of an enriched understanding of choices.

When one is influenced by anything, two things need to occur: one needs to pay attention to the object of attention and he/she needs to confirm and endorse the emergent propositional implication of the stated implicit or explicit parlance of the attention. For example, a player may fail to operate a successful string of action during a game and as he/she fails, his/her attention may highlight the failure and endorses that the so-called failure is an indication that he/she would fail in the second string of action too. As he/she corroborates the possibility of failing through reconfirming the failure, he/she will be more prone to fail as the occasion arises. This can happen in a few seconds and can be affected by sundry unconscious factors too. There are evidently numerous signs of automaticity and automatic behaviors within the context of this behavior. In other words, mindlessness can be tied to the dynamics of the failed operation through a recursive pattern of negativity, helplessness, and self-defeating statements.

In Langerian mindfulness, one is trained to become perceptive of the power of his/her choices in paying attention to the wide variety of stimuli. Analogically, when one is watching a TV program with an access to a remote control, one can be vigilantly reminded of one's power of changing the channel instead of getting stuck in one channel. Understanding the possibility of the power to change the channel lies at the center of Langerian mindfulness. When one is mindless, he/she is incarcerated within the context of his/her own perspective, namely the channel in this example and thus he/she cannot undertake any action other than what the already taken channel or perspective suggests.

The automatic lingering in a single perspective is energy consuming as it is gradually encapsulated within a tedious, monotonous, repetitive, and recursive mode of being. In order to emancipate oneself from the banal and rule-governed behavior and its synchronous fatigue, one is trained to practice shifting the attention from one thing to the other in a deliberate and meaningful way.

In Langerian mindfulness, therefore, one primarily learns to look at positive and new things in the realm of his/her being. This could be a new look at a friend or even oneself with a positive tone.

Starting everything afresh constitutes one of the main characteristics of Langerian mindfulness. As stale bread tastes dull and disengaging, a stale state of being is frustratingly disengaging too. As one experiences an active state of mind through a meaningful and sagacious search for novelty, the stale state of being is transformed into a delightful state of existentiality through a phenomenological connectedness to Langerian mindfulness.

Langerian mindfulness, thus, gives rise to a shift of perspective and language. The performer who is cooped and caged by self-defeating statements learns that he/she is constantly exposed to a series of choices. Thoughts are choices too. As one experiences the power of choice through changing the TV channel, one can experience the power of having a choice through learning to say yea or nay to a string of thoughts. Mindlessly shaped clusters of thoughts inscribe the certitude of apprehending possibility in a fixed form with unchangeable, unalterable, and indubitable layers of reality justified through the recursively unquestionable series of assumptions. Langerian mindfulness targets the fixation and its paramount legitimacy and calls for the possibility of going beyond the stability of the subjective propositional clinging.

The fixation is here meant to be both in the emotional, cognitive, and behavioral domains. So as psychoanalysis, cognitive psychology and behaviorists concentrate on demonstrating the paralyzing impacts of fixation in their own sphere of interest, Langerian mindfulness helps the performer understand the implications of a premature cognitive and emotional commitment and facilitates the process of reconciling with the emergent possibility of new modes of being.

When one is experiencing the automaticity of a behavior, one moves in the path of predetermined pavement of possibility delineated by schemas of the past. The performance in the pathway is enumerated by the kaleidoscopic-determined indexes of absolute, possible, and certain steps. If the movement transpires with an abidance by the rule governed dictum of possibility, the performance turns out to be maximized by virtue of the same identifiers of the operative possibility with the hegemonic context of possibility.

This will ultimately produce conceptualization of optimization based on the overall interpretive discourse of pre-defined realm of possibility. Hence, performance can flourish or consummate as much as the explication of possibility already determines the depth and width of possible optimization. The points of departure and points of successful landing are already elucidated within the scope of the known possibility. This may be similar to the current manifestation of transportation routes where the signs already indicate the permissibility or impermissibility of movements.

Langerian mindfulness changes the whole story here. Possibility is no longer possibility based on the known recursive conceptualization of possibility. In Langerian mindfulness, the known connectedness to the categorization of possibility and impossibility lies in the taxonomy of mindlessness. Langerian notion of possibility goes beyond the cognitive, computational, linear, analytical, and logical mode of possibility (see Fatemi, 2014).

The substantive transformation of conceptualization of possibility is idiosyncratic to Langerian mindfulness. It starts off with providing the performer with a discernment of broadening prism of possibility with no finite point of establishment. The performer here learns to realize the imprisoning implications of the finitely translated modes of possibility.

Langerian mindfulness leaps forward through providing the person with the perceptiveness of the creational competencies of one's inner potential. The leaping beyond the established modes of equations would emerge in the heart of preparatory move of Langerian mindfulness. The subtlety of the cognitive and emotional discernment of the infinite scope of possibility would allow the performer to briskly challenge the debilitating mindsets with their psychological and cognitive heftiness. The performer here learns to question and debate the validity and reliability of the existing debilitating mindsets as he/she learns to realize that mindsets can be choices and a repeatedly operative mindset is not necessarily the best choice to live with. Choices can be created as affluently as possible when the performer is in touch with three phenomenological states of being: tranquility and calmness, inner intimacy, and inner security.

Mindfulness facilities the possibility of implementing the three aforementioned stages of being: this occurs through developing a non-judgmental, open and flexible state of intrapersonal and interpersonal connectedness.

Calmness and tranquility would go away when the mind is mindlessly engaged in massiveness, multiplicity, and separation. Mindfulness is empowering as it helps the performer discern the empowering understanding of experiencing the authenticity of one's being. Langerian mindfulness challenges the idea of having a template for peak performance. Relying on a set of determining rules for performance would be in contrast with the uniqueness of performer and his/her exclusive sensibility. This does not purport the lambasting approach of Langerian mindfulness for helpful information in presenting the scientific understanding of different domains of performance which began with an in-depth look into cognition and its wide-ranging operations including sustained attention, selective attention, conflict monitoring, processing and storing information, decision making, planning, and problem solving. Effective utilization of the so called elite skills is taken into consideration in Langerian analysis of high-level performance.

When one finds the possibility of disengaging from the paralyzing compartmentalization of automatic conceptualizations, one would embrace the courage to take upon himself/herself to initiate the first action of creation. The creation espouses the wholeness and the synchronicity of the performer and the performance in that it propounds a synergy between the work and the creator. The creator's psychological connectedness to the object of creation expedites the process of a present oriented focus on the present time. It serves as a preamble for the optimal cognitive preparation too since it nourishes the performer with a non-judgmental based equanimity under pressure, a comprehensive sense of inner intimacy and inner comfort and an open stage of flexibility with manifestation in response styles.

Mindful-based performance is inspired to unlock the cognitive and emotional structures while creating new avenues and alternative ways of exploring the possibility. In doing so, the performer is ontologically connected to the experiential process of seeking psychological possibility through the infinitely operative source of possibility. Langerian mindfulness unleashes the possibility of possible examination of creative possibilities in novel cognitive and emotional domains with their behavioral implications.

Langerian mindfulness targets the absence in our daily life and presents strategies to enhance the connectedness to the moment. This being absent in the moment instead of being present is entrenched within the automatically learned behaviors that do not allow the performer to go outside the boxes: "as we blindly follow routines or unwittingly carry out senseless orders, we are acting like automatons, with potentially grace consequences for ourselves and others" Langer, 1989, p. 4). The key in Langerian mindfulness is to welcome the possibility of a new perspective (Langer, 2009, 2005, 1997, 1985, 1987).

As soon as we commit ourselves to some established form of information and we lock ourselves into a specific mode of thinking, Langerian mindfulness argues, we would deprive ourselves of seeking novel ways or alternative modes of thinking. In Langerian mindfulness, we actively restructure our mindsets through the creation of new categories or distinctions (Langer, 1989, p. 4).

Performance can be analyzed into two different modes of action: one as something that lies in the array of automatic forms of thinking and one as something creational that is created by the performer as the creator. The former is mostly associated with activities and undertakings that are subsumed under a category with multiple forms of labels such as job, occupation, chores, etc. whereas the latter is born in the heart of a productive form of action known as work. In other words, the first one may be done in accordance with the domination of the previously prescriptive modes of thinking in the context of doing something for the sake of its mere implementation.

The second is coupled with an act of creation where the performer finds himself/herself as a creator and the creational relationship between the creation and the creator espouses a unique relationship. This relationship is characterized through belonging, love, fervor, and unity.

The creator is unified with the creation and thus wholeness is an emergent state which unfolds itself in the process of the creation.

Langerian mindfulness (see, Langer, 2009, 2005, 1997, 1985, 1987, etc.) would offer the following features in enhancing the richness of a performance:

1. A proactive engagement in the moment whereby the performer is consummately engaged in the activity.
2. The engagement is associated with noticing new things. The search for novelty occurs at the apogee of the connectedness to the moment.
3. Connectedness grows out of the unifying interaction of the performer with the performance.
4. The unification provides the performer with an experiential process of wholeness.
5. Wholeness and health embrace one another with the activation of multifarious cognitive, emotional, and behavioral components of the performer.
6. Multiplicity, massiveness, automaticity, and masquerading of the self are replaced by unification, wholeness, mindfulness, and authenticity. This helps the performer phenomenologically experience the process of "being there."
7. With an increase of the scope of mindfulness, one would experience the power of choices through the interactive process of being both an observer and an actor.
8. The expansive mode of mindfulness and its ontological implications would allow the performer to realize the distinction between the physiological and the existential presentation of the performance-oriented features: I feel anger or I feel sadness are different from I am angry or I am sad, where in the first cluster of propositions the performer is separate from the feeling while in the translation of the second cluster of propositions the performer may existentially identify with the feeling, thus the performer may be emotionally in the language of Goleman "kidnapped" by the mindlessness of the emotion.
9. The power of choices would emerge with an increase of mindfulness whereby the performer comes to realize how his/her choices in the moment can create different types of reality. Understand-

ing the context would help the performer mindfully compose the context through a perspicacious sensitivity toward the context.

10. Mindfulness would espouse creativity. A mindful performer is not encapsulated in the templates of the prescribed perspectives. If he/she remains there, he/she would deprive himself/herself of an authentic engagement in the moment. The eyes transfixed in the mirrors of the past would alienate themselves from a genuine indulgence in the windows of the presence. Thus, the operative self with a subjugation to the past stricken sovereignty would happen to end up in the cul de sac of pretentiousness, superciliousness, and bogusness.
11. Performance in line with automaticity would eventually give rise to a rupture between the context and the performer whereas a mindful performance would encourage rapture in the emergent action of mindful engagement.
12. Performance in the context of absence-oriented connectedness would impose a sole search for pre-identified realms of possibilities.
13. Langerian mindfulness activates the search for liminal spaces where the unidentified spaces are incessantly available with their potential horizons of possibilities.
14. Mindfulness in its Langerian context would facilitate the process of maximizing one's performance.

When it comes to work performance, the word "work" often reminds people of something strenuous, stress oriented, tedious, and monotonous. There tends to be a dichotomy between work-oriented activities and leisure-oriented undertakings. Even in a number of psychological models including Eric Bern's Transactional Analysis, spontaneous ego state is mostly associated with activities that may appear to transpire mostly in out-of-office activities.

The expressions people use to describe "coolness" are largely coupled with enterprises that occur outside the stringently serious realms of job. It, thus, may be safe to say that work and life may dramatically move in line in opposite directions if not in contradictory status. This has been historically vociferated in Karl Marx's clamorous contention that works and working conditions impose not only estrangement but also espouse alienation for workers to the extent that they lose their identity.

The worker's life is therefore purported to be far from the real taste of life. To dissipate the burden of work from life and to eliminate the alienation of self from work, scholars have often suggested the work life balance where the imbalance caused by the forcible tension of work and life would disappear and the balance be established as a panacea to reconcile both and personal life situations.

While the balance between life and work has given rise to promising chapters in human interactions and has contributed to facilitating the betterment of life, it intrinsically suggests a clandestine assumption of bipolar category which potentially stand against one another. The ground-breaking findings of Langer's forty year-long scholarly research presents surprising results and brings about unexpectedly exquisite news about the relationship between work and life.

Langerian Mindfulness propounds that instead of work-life-balance perspective, the work-life integration may lead us to a happier and more prosperous life with opulently rich results in the realm of our work. Langerian doctrine suggests that work-life-balance perspective, albeit helpful and valuable in its own context, may develop a split of self in that the self at work may be translated in dramatically different modes than the self at home. This is not meant to be a recapitulation of split personality, double-bind personality or multiple personality concept in its clinical term as you may have seen that in the movies *Three Faces of Eve* or *Dr. Jekyll and Mr. Hyde* but it enunciates a drastic connection between two ways of being which may boil down to a lack of connectedness to the wholeness of personality. Again, one needs to warn that the work-life integration in Langerian Mindfulness is not meant to nullify the manifestation of different roles: it is not expected that a CEO goes home and treats his/her family members in the hierarchical order of organizational chain, nor does one expect that an officer goes home and by whistling summons up his kids as you may recall that sort of approach in *The Sound of Music*.

Langerian Doctrine proposes that wholeness and health are walking arm-in-arm: it is interesting to know that etymologically the word "health" and "whole" come from the same root. Once you lose your wholeness, your health would be jeopardized and as you get far from being healthy, your wholeness disappears. Langerian Mindfulness argues for a praxis where the integration of work and life conditions can consummate one's way of being. The integration calls for a phenomenological connectedness to the present moment in that one may consciously notice new things and look for novelty whether at home or work. The reason behind fatigue at work or at home, Langerian Mindfulness argues, is because of the sovereignty of mundane, quotidian, banal, and routinized engagements.

The work-life integration perspective would suggest that one can keep his/her perceptive consciousness alive in the moment and through practicing this liveliness would savor the pleasure both at work and at home. When one learns to live mindfully and implement mindfulness in both work and home, one would experience the exhilarating joy of both in his/her lived experiences. Through tons of experimental research, Langerian Mindfulness has substantiated the possibility of an experiential change in one's mode of being. Thus, Langerian Mindfulness demonstrates that mindfulness can promise a transformation of being: it is not just about cognition; it is about a new mode of being. The novel consummation of work and life experiences would augur the interplay of work and home connectedness in their underlying existential components. One's existence can be mindfully linked to both realms of activities whether at work or home once the existence is nourished through the gift of mindfulness. Langerian Mindfulness presents techniques and skills that can enhance the comprehensive interactive process of synergy between work and home. The integrative work and life experiences would give not only a healthier way of being but also produce a more brilliant performance at work.

Langerian mindfulness opens up infinite possibilities for discovering liminal spaces in the process of performing the presence-oriented performance.

7

MINDFULNESS AND LEARNING

When people are educationally and socially exposed to recursive modes of thinking and emotions, they would most likely follow the priming of the suggested frameworks. The process propounds the acceptance of a series of assumptions that are unquestionably solid and reliable.

The epistemological exploration of the content of learning induces mindlessness with a focus on fixed relationships.

Emergence of priming, mapping, cognitive models, assimilation, accommodation, and such like past stricken concepts within learning strategies, therapeutics interventions, and pedagogical approaches may justify the attempt for providing a structured framework where sensibility of senses needs to be determined on the strength of their proximity and adjacency to the introduced modes of mindsets.

Established contents of understanding, knowing, and learning would propound a fairly stable agenda for learning and teaching, curriculum planning, and policy making. This would have a rather stringent emphasis on abiding by the pre-identified ways of learning. This may have huge implications for the sensibility of senses in the world of education. Apart from the monolithic perspective of some educators in ostracizing the application of senses without a direct linkage to the prescribed text, some others have been mainly enmeshed within the application of senses with a focus on the past. This, albeit fruitful and helpful, in expressing the personally lived experiences, has reinforced the tendency of the sensibility of senses within the paradigmatic analysis of the past.

If one's experiential process of lived experiences is led to gain sensibility through the paramount sovereignty of sensibility within the top-down processing of mindless programs, how can he/she phenomenologically relate to his/her sense of presence mindfully?

Approaches on senses and sensing have been mainly inspired and affected by psychological perspectives where the initial focus has discussed the stimulation of receptor cells and the process of information transmission to the brain centers. The presentations of the absolute threshold and the difference threshold within neurophysiological and psychological research and their implications have examined how the amount of stimulation may have an influence on the psychological experience of the stimuli.

The discussions have concentrated on the pathways between the five senses namely vision, hearing, smell, touch, and taste and the specific areas on the brain. Accordingly seeing a flower in the garden, for example, can be attributed to the electrical activation of the primary visual cortex in the occipital lobes of the brain as the hearing sensation may be ascribed to the activation of the auditory complex in the temporal lobes. Meanings to the sensations have also been discussed in the framework of perceptions where interpretations of the experience have become distinct from the mere process of sensation.

The configuration of psychological research on sensation and perception and their discussion of senses seem to have been implicitly embedded within a look into the past: the prior knowledge, the schema, the accessibility to previous exposure, the search for a repertoire that must have been already established.

Deregowski, Muldrow, and Muldrow (1972), for instance, demonstrated that how the sense of vision and the perception of pictures need to be related to the people's past educational and socialization experiences. The people of Mekan in Ethiopia who seemingly had no previous education and had not been exposed to pictures could hardly identify the picture of animals that were presented to them. In a more recent example, Sporer, Trinkl, and Guberova (2007) indicated that Turkish-born children in Europe were faster than the Austrian children in matching the faces of Turkish people. The research displayed no difference in perception when it came to the matching of German faces. Both groups, namely Turkish and Austrian, matched the German faces equally fast.

People may be encouraged to be well attuned to their senses and be willing and prepared to express and create avenues through which the content of particular senses manifests themselves. While this notion of sense expressiveness and its experiential sedimentation would help people be more effectively in touch with their own positions and experience more empowerment, it could go one-sided if it cannot generate novel and innovative forms of expressiveness. A past-based sensual mode of expressiveness would be ultimately bound by the same textual determinacy.

Challenging the determinacy of the established phenomenological cognitive and emotional registration, Langer (1997) writes:

> From time to time educators attempt to recognize the fluidity of knowledge by providing students with a list of the pros and cons of a particular idea or theory. Much as a physician might list the potential negative side effects along with the expected benefits of a treatment, critical thinking is sometimes taught in schools by having students list the advantages and disadvantages of a controversial idea. Such an exercise almost invariably falls short of the recognition that each potential benefit may also be a liability and that a disadvantage may become an advantage. (p. 134)

The determinacy of the established phenomenological cognitive and emotional registration and its plausibility may emanate from the etiological goal of knowledge as the hegemony and mastery. Deep inside the concept of the very mastery, there lies an urge for certainty which unfolds itself in the process of knowing. The encouragement of the commitment toward emotional and cognitive registered modes and their phenomenological preference would entangle the senses within an introduced top-down processing. This would also expand a past seeking predisposition to gain sensibility.

On challenging the domineering implications of such plausibility and sensibility, Langer (1997) posits that

> Although the proliferation of dimensions of intelligence may help prop up students' sense of self-worth, in the process of indentifying strengths as may be unintentionally undermining students' develop-

> ment. Not only do students who are helped lost the potential benefit of generating a view of their own abilities, but the recipients of most remedial efforts usually accept a devaluation of self. Such devaluation sometimes causes people to compensate by devaluating others. In other words, people accept the ways others have been shown to be better than they by identifying ways in which they are better than others. Adding dimensions of intelligence encourages such labeling and competition. (p. 136)

The established sense of plausibility and sensibility within Western framework is inextricably tied to the scientific rigor of the natural sciences and their implications for human and social sciences. Deep down the prescribed methods and approaches within the phenomenological plausibility as planned, there lies the idea of a scientific truth that needs to be promoted. The modes of expressiveness, thus, need to gain their sensibility within the pre-established paradigms. The emphasis, again, is on the structured, organized, and composed models from the past; the tendency to look for the fit between what is and the schema of the scientific models.

Challenging the hegemony of the scientific model as the deciding factor in our modes of living and being, Spariosou (2004) writes:

> We might possess "the best" scientific theory, such as deep ecology, the "best" information and communication technology, such as digital and quantum computers, or the "best" political system, such as democracy. And yet, we may end up putting them all to inappropriate and counterproductive uses, as we have seen happen repeatedly throughout the history of scientific and technological development, as well as the history of world politics. (p. 21)

When sensibility is quested in the abode of the established structures and models as defined by scienticism, there would be an attempt to compare the expressed ways of the youths with the plausible modes of correspondence within the structural schema of the past: it should fit the big Text of expressiveness to make sense. Therefore, one may see the ineluctable manifestation of an approach toward what has already been established.

Parents and teachers' preoccupation, moving in line with the established phenomenology, would, thus, be a concern about the youth's match with the pre-organized system of schemas and scripts. Cognition is more concentrated on factors that induce the compatibility with the pre-existing models. The modes of expressiveness, albeit creative, are necessarily promoted with a tilt toward the hegemony of the schemas of the past or what is pervasively introduced through the powerful societal, educational, and political medium.

The endorsement of registration within the cognitive and emotional top down phenomenology would end up "stuffing" youths with numerous forms of mapping that are inextricably connected to the hegemony of a prescribed mindset. The assumptions here indicate that there is a text that needs to be abided by, that needs to be implemented, and that needs to serve as the illuminating source for action. The Text in the prescribed top down phenomenology as established eschews from fluidity and transformation since any change in the structural patterns of the leading Text would contradict the implementation and application of the Text.

Questioning the hegemony of this indulgence in the scientific infatuation, Gardner (2006) indicates:

> What sense would we make of the greatest work of art or literature, or the most important religious or political ideas, or the most enduring puzzles about the meaning of life and death, if we only thought of them in the manner of a scientific study or proof? If all we did was quantify? What political or business leader would be credible, at the time of crisis, if all he could do was offer scientific explanations or mathematical proofs, if he could not address the hearts of his audience? The great physicist Niels Bohr once mused on this irony: "there are two kinds of truth, deep truth and shallow truth, and the function of Science is to eliminate the deep truth." (p. 15)

Notwithstanding the fruitful applicability of the schematic structures associated with the scientific rigor for youth's wellness, the discourse of registration within the top-down processing of the prescriptive modes of expressiveness as a contingency for sensibility would limit the emotional and cognitive modes of expressiveness and their affective phenomenological influences. Sensual modes of expressiveness would, therefore, fall into two categories: the past-based sensual modes of expressiveness where the expressiveness is placed in a connectedness to the schematic structures of the pre-established models. This way, the senses namely vision, hearing, smell, touch, and taste can have their own modes of expressiveness. Nonetheless, because of the top-down processing nature of the discourse of sensibility, sundry modes of expressiveness would need to pass through the filters with a conspicuous reliance on the pre-established schematic structures.

Learners, albeit active in this mode of expressiveness, would largely depend on reference points that define sensibility of sensual expressiveness by virtue of the flux of the previously made structures. In other words, sensual expressiveness would turn out to be in the language of Langer (1989) mindlessness that is operating from a single perspective enmeshed in "the premature cognitive commitment" of the past.

Mindlessness-based sensual registration, although it uses senses and their plethora of benefits in its programs, would suggest a monolithic perspective that ultimately seek the connectedness to the schematic structures of the past as the criteria for viability and reliability.

As the avenues of knowing and understanding are contained more in the pre-identified chapters of schematic analysis of the past, they tend to dictate what to think and how to think in accordance with the syntagmatic analysis of the hegemony of the previously acquired modes of expressiveness. There would hardly be novelty, creativity, and innovation in a trail where the repetition of the frequently appeared schemas prescribe certain plausible modes of thinking and expressiveness. The phenomenologically created texts designed by mindless-based sensual registration may be distinct from the text created by the pervasive non-sensual presentation, yet, they would limit the possibilities and circumscribe the horizons of expressiveness as they merely substantiate themselves through the past-stricken approach of top-down sensibility.

The phenomenologically mindless-based modes of cognitive and emotional expressiveness would move in the framework of a reductionism which seems to be the corollary of the scientific infatuation.

Deep down the position of knowing as the leading factor of the mindless-based phenomenology, the notion of certainty unfolds itself. The textual and sensual cognitive and emotional phenomenology would be both abortive as long as they linger in the stability of the mindlessly repeated schematic analysis. The youths, in both cases, would express themselves in line with a series of repetition, organization, and structures that resonate with the pre-existing patterns.

Challenging this position of certitude and certainty and calling for the fluidity of living in the moment through observing new things and learning exquisite modes of beings and becoming, Langer (2009) writes:

> Certainty is a cruel mindset. It hardens our minds against possibility and closes them to the world we actually live in. When all is certain, there are no choices for us. If there is no doubt, there is no choice. When we are certain, we are blind to the uncertainties of the world whether we recognize it or not. It is uncertainty that we need to embrace. (pp. 24–25)

Mindful creativity openly creates possibilities and avidly looks for newness within the modes of expressiveness and the things of the expressed. The art-based phenomenology for youths which may be the translation of one form of mindful expressiveness can also depart from mindlessness and proactively and mindfully create possibilities or can be plagued with the tyranny of the prescriptive modes of schematic analysis thus proceeding within the realm of mindlessness. The enhancement of possibilities in the heart of mindfulness would help the mindful expressiveness explore the realm of sensibility beyond the predetermined scripts of certainty. This can facilitate the process of transcending the commonly accepted forms of sensation and perception.

The fluidity of creative mindfulness would enrich the indeterminacy of creative expressiveness and would promise the possibility of self-creation through the expansion of choices. This would enlighten how the political, personal, and cultural position of people can be enlivened through a recondite discovery of the relationship between the modes of expressiveness and the search for new possibilities of exploration.

For the question of "is" and "ought," Langer proposes that a large number of unquestionably accepted series of "ought" are embroiled within the mindlessly prompted single perspective that has been espoused and reinforced on the strength of socially constructed realities. The tyranny of social constructions has been so overwhelmingly powerful to dictate and impose a specific language for mind operation. The mind operating on this level of influence has been socially, culturally, and politically shaped through the maximizing power of mindsets with pre-determined agendas of mindlessness.

In other words, the relationship between repetition, exposure, habituation, and familiarity has frequently prescribed and proscribed certain modes of cogitation with implications for behaviors, feelings, and thoughts.

The chain of familiarity and contemplation have perpetuated an entanglement within the top-down processing where the mind is constricted by the strength of experientially created modes of behavior, thoughts, and feelings.

Langer argues that this top-down processing deprives mind of innovative leaps and leads into the cul-de-sac of mindlessness. To Langer, a focus on the previously established behavioral, emotional, and cognitive mechanisms of the experience impedes the process of a connection to the experiences of "now."

Langerian mindfulness encourages a turn from the absolutism of propositions to contingencies of parlance. Mind trapped in the priming of certitude, Langer argues, is inclined to stagnate. Central to Langerian mindfulness lies a rigorous attention toward a contextual perceptiveness of situational awareness. Langer delineates that a mind free of context would voyage in the oscillating waves of cognitive and emotional fallacies.

Langer explicates the potential competencies of a mind brimming with infinitely creative possibilities. Evaluation appears to be a blockage in embracing emancipation both at intellectual and emotional levels. The maximization of the past and its decisive impact in narrating the present moment limits and circumscribes the mind from experiencing the liminal spaces where the novelty of looking into the unknown brings a revolutionizing paradigm for the present moment.

To Langer, mind and presence are essentially necessary for delving into composure, tranquility, and happiness. A mind overwhelmed with multiplicities, acceleration, and massiveness falls into a pathologically established state of absence. The absence-oriented mind is scattered and sporadic with a loss of focus. The presence-oriented mind sits comfortably in the proactive stage of contemplation. A presence-oriented mind, thus, consciously experiences the connectedness from which perspicacity, delicacy, and sagacity of mindful morality arise, assisting the actor in an examination of any given "ought" in the praxis of propositional implications.

From a Langerian perspective, legality may often lead to immorality: Rules are not handed down from heaven, they are decisions made by people and people and decisions are bound by time and spaces. With a mere focus on rules and regulations, people may find themselves constricted in paying attention to the underpinnings of moral contexts. Mindfulness does not negate and nullify laws and legalities, but, instead of prescribing a rule-governed life, it opens up a path of exploration for a rule-guided life. By mindlessly following laws people become blind to morality.

To Langer, mindfulness is not just about cognition; it is a shift of being that occurs when one experiences a recondite change in one's ontology. The experience is characterized by proactive intentionality to look into the unfamiliar while immersed in the familiar. The mind here goes beyond the predefined boundaries of thinking and scrutinizes the possibility of otherwise in the well-known endorsement of the status quo. This opens up sundry extensions of possibilities with a break from the manacles of premature cognitive commitments.

8

MINDFUL PHENOMENOLOGY

Phenomenology focuses on lived experiences. One's perspective is largely built based on his/her lived experiences to the extent that the process and the nature of the experience may have a huge impact on one's level of connectedness to the world. It was Husserl who first presented phenomenology and concentrated on the meaning of the experience. The question for him and phenomenological psychologists concerns the meaning of the experience.

With the introduction of intentionality, Husserl developed an ineluctably established relationship between consciousness and its subject to the effect that the noema or noematic correlate (what is experienced) is essentially correlated to noesis, or noetic correlate (the way it is experienced). In line with understanding intentionality as a significant component of phenomenology, the distinction between transcendental phenomenology and existential phenomenology may help us understand how the role of the observer and the actor may be differently delineated in each: in transcendental phenomenology the possibility of going beyond the experience and getting detached from the experience is possible whereas in existential phenomenology the possibility of the disentanglement does not exist. In other words, the existential phenomenology argues for the inseparability of our presuppositions. The complete *epoche* or bracketing may not be possible according to existential phenomenologists including Heidegger, Sartre, and Merleau-Ponty contrary to transcendental phenomenologists led by Husserl. The latter underlines the possibility of transcending one's experience so much so that you can see the experience differently.

While looking at the experience and the way it is experienced, we may become more interested in understanding the levels of experience and how they may unfold themselves.

The experience may focus on the cognitive level and therefore the way it is experienced may activate the cognitive oriented channels. When you are in an interlocutory communication on understanding and deciphering some meaning in a parlance, your experience may be mainly embedded in the cognitive level. Inter-subjectivity refers to this level of experience where understanding revolves around the cognitive excavation of what takes place in a reciprocal influence. If you are engaged in a conversation or have a presentation on Heisenberg's Uncertainty, the experience may be associated with a level of awareness where you delve into decoding the meaning of the interaction through using preconceived signs and concepts. This will also be embedded in a bilateral and reciprocal give and take as to the cognitive domain of the interactive process. When people fail to partake in an intersubjective simultaneity, there will be gaps that keep them apart in terms of the cognition level.

In the meantime, there can be a level of experience where the two interlocutors embrace and experience an emotional bond or an affect attunement where the experience is no longer operative in merely a cognitive level but it includes an emotional engagement where the two people experience an emotional connection. This level of experience has been studied in terms of cognitive science too and has been termed as brain to brain coupling.

I use the term "inter-subjectivity" here beyond the psychotherapeutic and psychoanalytic contexts where the focus is on the reciprocal relationship between two minds and its therapeutic configuration.

In both the intersubjective and the attunement levels, there can be varying degrees of mindfulness. Essentially the intersubjective and the attunement levels are interwoven together in a therapeutic context but for the sake of clarification, I posit that an interaction can move in two different directions although these directions may ultimately boil into one horizon if mindfulness occurs.

You may go through a discussion on prices with a colleague and your direction may merely go around the exchange of information with cognitive levels of involvement. This, in the meantime, may be associated with an encounter where the two interactors iterate not only the cognitive sphere of their interaction but also the emotional level of their togetherness.

One might suggest that there will always be a dialectics of the emotional and cognitive engagement in a dyad, albeit hidden, tacit or marginal. However, the horizontalization of the emotional and cognitive levels can vary. Horizontalization stands versus verticalization here. The former takes into consideration all possible emergent meanings and examining and elucidating their multiple meanings whereas the latter highlights the importance and significance of some specific meanings based on the pre-established paradigms of the so-called natural attitude.

In Langerian phenomenology, natural attitude is interwoven with mindlessness where acting from a single perspective or a repeatedly induced mindset would develop automatic responses and behaviors where reflecting on the experience and the reflexivity regarding the experience seldom occur.

Imaginative variation or imaginative free variation in phenomenology may move in line with Langerian emphasis on celebrating multiple perspectives.

Langerian phenomenological mindfulness here underlines the interactive relationship between the observer and the actor. A mere emphasis on the role of the observer may lead to different forms of mindlessness where the reality of the actor and the actor's experience can be concealed to total oblivion.

In the meantime, there are scholars who indicate that all information processing is essentially emotional. Thus, any cognitive interaction can ultimately boil down to an emotional level.

Whether we comply with the distinction between attunement and inter-subjectivity or bring all of the mental processing under the incessantly ubiquitous flux of emotions, the question from a Langerian mindfulness would address whether the state of mind is passively subdued to the inundation of either cognitive or emotional mechanisms to the extent that the experience of the moment is overshadowed by the maximization of the cognitive or emotional prompts of the past.

As long as the past over determines the present, the experience and the expression of the moment is subjugated to the sovereignty of mindlessness.

9

LEVELS OF MINDFULNESS

If mindfulness unfolds itself in a proactive state of mind where living in the moment is experienced away from the governing hue and cry of the schemas and priming of mental models, one may be mindfulness in one context and mindless in another one.

In the meantime, there can be different degrees of mindfulness when it comes to interpersonal relationships.

In order to examine different levels of mindfulness, let's scrutinize sundry modes of beings in an interaction.

You may be cognitively aware of what the other person is communicating without being in touch with his/her emotional domains. This may happen when someone is solely aware of your words and understands them in terms of denotation but cannot relate to you and cannot reach you emotionally. The result is lack of empathy. This level of being takes place in the information level where people exchange information for the sake of conducting a communication but there is no soul in the interaction. Examples of this type of being can be perceptible in family relations where people are physically beside one another but at the same time they experience a lack of emotional and psychological being.

This level is subsumed under mindlessness where being is propositionally there.

Imagine that you have been on a bus for a long trip. The bus ride has not been satisfactory at all and you have had a hard time feeling comfortable while being on the ride.

Upon arrival into your destination and as soon as you get off the bus, your awaiting friend who has come to pick you up bursts into words and his initiating words say: "You could have flown. Let me show you in my I-phone that you could have paid the same price while flying instead of going through the hardship of the bus ride."

This response may have been as equally disturbing as the experience with the bus. The friend's response is indicative of an example of mindlessness where instead of examining your perspective and its underlying needs, the respondent comes up with a response based on his repertoire of advice.

Examples of this type of mindlessness can be affluently found in family relationships, corporate life, and other extended interpersonal relationships.

Mindfulness nourishes an intentional, open, curious, creative, and flexible attention toward the other one in an interaction. This attention demonstrates that the other is not considered as an object or a thing.

Thingness is the beginning of injustice, oppression, encroachment of rights and abrasive, abusive and aggressive behavior. Mindlessness is thus the cornerstone of social malaise where the being of the other is compartmentalized in accordance with one's monolithic singled sides viewpoint. This view may ignore, disregard, deride the being of the other.

Mindfulness legitimizes the being of the other without equating the legitimacy of the being of the actor to the unquestionable identification with the perspective of the observer.

Your mindfulness requires you to go beyond the cognitive level of what is being heard and search for the underlying emotional configuration. An indulgence in one's perspective may hamper the possibility of paying attention to alternative interpretative modes. This is often associated with a dogmatic insistence on having access to the right information.

Langerian perspective places a huge emphasis on accessing the phenomenological experience of the other to ensure the possibility of creating a bridge in the context of a locutionary act.

Now imagine that you have a grandmother who is hard at hearing and you go to visit her. You love her dearly and you both have a strong emotional attachment. If you choose to discuss with her concepts which require high cognitive involvement, your communication will lose its vivacity and livelihood since she may not demonstrate a proactive being in response to your queries. Nonetheless, if you bring topics that are of mutual interest from an emotional perspective, you both experience a more mindful being in terms of your relationship in this scenario.

Here you have different levels of operative beings: in one level, your being is there but not really there and in another one you may experience a more lucid form of being with strong engagement.

In intercultural mindfulness, one needs to enhance his/her familiarity with the other's experience and the expression of that experience to be able to step into his/her realm of meaning making and sensibility.

Enhancing one's intercultural and interpersonal competencies may require an in-depth understanding of the underlying cognitive and emotional components of one's behavior and its psychological context.

Mindfulness entails intentionality in that it modulates, organizes, amplifies, attenuates, regulates, rectifies, and coordinates attention. The mode of being has a lot to do with the mode of attention. When attention is sporadically diffused or stranded, one's being ceases to display its centrality.

Mindfulness requires a deliberate focus on the here and now. It necessitates an intentional, open, curious, caring, and flexible propensity toward exploring what may unfold itself in the moment.

This may stand in opposition to the constricting components that appear in the way of creating mindfulness.

Understanding the difference between absolute propositions and conditional propositions and exploring the differences between certitude and contingency and their psychological implications help one increase the level of mindfulness.

If in looking at an object we come up with an assertion that this is a bottle of water, it espouses implications quite different from articulating that this can be a bottle of water. The former freezes reality of the object whereas the latter opens it up to numerous possibilities where the object can be so many things including a bottle of water amongst so many other things including a pencil holder, a vase, etc.

Understanding the difference would help one to examine the realm of his/her possibilities beyond the given set of his/her assumptions. This would enable one to see how his/her choices can go beyond the established set of contexts that he/she is embedded in.

This perceptiveness would help people to see how social construction of realities can be revisited and can be deconstructed. In a personal level, it allows one to see how he/she can revamp his/her narratives and discover his/her own voice through distancing from the absoluteness of what one has been given and looking for alternative modes of composing his/her new narratives.

Authenticity transpires in the heart of mindfulness. People can be forcibly lost in the meanders of pretentiousness and ostentatious personas.

Langerian studies have demonstrated that even animals, including dolphins, can tell the difference between an ostentatious mode of being and an authentic presentation. Mindfulness would help people to be in touch with themselves without being afraid or anxious. An increase of mindfulness at this stage would help people discover the importance of their own agency instead of over-dependency on the good opinion of others.

This would give rise to emotional development where people also become authentically sensitive toward their party's needs, desires, concerns, and wants. This sensitivity is aligned with openness and flexibility in decoding non-verbal signs and preparing the suitable responses. An authentic being grows in line with mindfulness which entails a non-evaluative approach with a caring attitude toward the other.

Attention to variability enhances the scope of mindfulness.

Paying attention to variability would allow people to deal with stressful situations in a more effective manner. Langerian mindfulness would argue that *no one is always anything.* For instance, no one is always depressed. No forms of beings are unchangeably fixed. There are times that one may be depressed or semi-depressed or not depressed even when he/she has been labeled as depressed.

The question from a Langerian phenomenological perspective is: what are the circumstances that make you depressed and what are the situations or factors that can be elicited to make you not depressed? When our attention is mindlessly fixed at one thing and is not flexibly moving toward another possible span of attention, we would get ourselves locked into unquestionable positions. Questioning this unquestionability would emerge in the heart of Langerian mindfulness.

One is encouraged to learn how learning about attention and its variability would help him/her see their power of managing their attention.

An enriched mode of mindfulness would develop detachment. When you are able to take off your watch and place it in front of your eyes, it vividly tells you that the act of separating the watch would suggest that you are not equated with your watch.

This stage of being and observing its detachments may be applied to detaching thoughts and sensations too. The detachment may indicate how an indulgence in one's own recursive thoughts would generate a subjective image where mindlessness resides. With an increase of heighted mindfulness, one learns how to mindfully experience a detachment from his/her own subjectivity including his/her own thoughts, assumptions, and mindsets.

The power of choices grows in the spirit of mindfulness. From a Langerian mindfulness perspective, anxiety is a choice. An increase of mindfulness and its implications would help one see how he/she can shift from an automatic mode or behavior namely mindlessness to mindfulness. This shift would illustrate how choices can be sensibly celebrated through an act of mindfulness and its call for exploring novel things.

This stage of being helps one examine moment by moment the possibility of making choices instead of abiding by an automatically learned behavior. Every morning, one may automatically go for an orange juice instead of pondering that this is a choice among so many other choices. Mindfulness brings an empowerment in that it helps one to exercise the power of choices and see how choices are plentiful.

An enhanced level of mindfulness suggests that we have far more control over our health than people now realize.

Langerian mindfulness also argues that, with an increase of mindfulness, people experience higher degrees of inter-subjectivity and attunement. Inter-subjectivity happens when people are simultaneously in the same cognitive mode, and attunement occurs when people are concurrently in the same emotional mode. Emotional dumbness, emotional deafness, and emotional blindness are the corollary of mindlessness where beings are far from wholeness.

With an increase of mindfulness, people can embrace a mind where peace is prevalent in both cognitive and emotional as well as behavioral domains. Mindlessly driven control emanates from anxiety, whereas mindfully driven control (in a Langerian version) stems from proactivity. Langerian mindfulness proposes that, with an increase of global mindfulness, mindlessly driven control is replaced by a proactive sense of togetherness, synergy, and sensitivity to the possibility of multiple perspectives. Mindlessly driven control engenders anxiety and instills protectiveness to defend one from the anxiety. Mindfully driven management (and not control in its pervasive sense) promotes understanding, empathy, and openness to celebrating the sensibility and plausibility of perspectives that may not make sense in the context of controlling mindlessness.

Ontological analysis of mindfulness would illustrate how one can be stuck in the tyrannical subjugation of the past with the denial of the power of choices for here and now. The illustration would demonstrate how the past and the future are both voids in that they do not exist.

From a mindful perspective, life unfolds itself in its vivacious mode in here and now and appreciating the availability of choices in the present moment would facilitate the power of empowerment in discerning the ability to choose. What mindfulness does is the elucidation of the novel, new and fresh complexions of the moment with their potential cynosures of numerous possibilities.

Mindfulness opens up the way to enhance the realm of actualization through explicating the domains of creativity. In the mindless mode, the state of mind is embroiled within pre-defined parameters of actualization and thus exquisite potentials are not manifesting their beings.

Heightened states of mindfulness would expand sundry horizons of meaning making and sensibility in their broadest prism of beings and allow the possibility of intermingling horizons, albeit far from one another, into creating a fusion of horizons.

The fusion of horizons may seem paradoxical or non-sensible for the state of mindlessness where relationships need to borrow their plausibility from the familiar orientation in a linear fashion.

Mindfulness in its enhanced ontologically multidimensional demonstration would substantiate the agency of the mind in serving as the sine quo non component of decision making.

The shift from the knowing mode to the understanding mode and the epistemic status to the ontological status appears to be at the apex of the radical transformation of consciousness in the process of reaching each stage of mindfulness as a more developed state of being with higher levels of emotional, cognitive, behavioral expansion.

This ontological expansion would serve as the key to reach the exploratory stage of understanding both the self and the other in the dialectical process of being and becoming.

The being in each stage is flexibly open for experiencing the subsequent becoming which in itself is readily available to undergo on purpose for the next stage thus serving both as a being and a becoming stage in the meantime with two different predicate levels.

Expression of the experience in each stage is infinitely accessible in the latitudinal connectedness of the mindful creativity.

REFERENCES

Albee, G. W. (1981). *Politics, power, prevention, and social change*. In J. M. Joffee and G. W. Albee (Eds.), Prevention through political action and social change (pp. 5–25). Hanover, NH: University Press of New England.

Allport, G. W. (1955). *Becoming: Basic considerations for a psychology of personality*. New Haven, CT: Yale University Press.

Bandura, A. (1977a). *Social learning theory*. Englewood Cliffs, NJ: Prentice Hall.

———. (1977b). Self efficacy: Toward a unifying theory of behavioral change. *Psychological Review*, 84, 191–215.

Banister, P., Burman, E., Parker, I., Taylor. M., and Tindall, C. (1994). *Qualitative methods in psychology: a research guide*. Buckingham, UK: Open University Press.

Bruner, J. (1986). *Actual minds, possible worlds*. Cambridge, MA: Harvard University Press.

Burger, J. M. (1992). *Desire for control: Personality, social, and clinical perspectives*. New York: Plenum.

Churchland, P. (1987). *Matter and consciousness: An introduction to the philosophy of mind*. Cambridge, MA: MIT Press.

Crum, A., and Lyddy, C. (2014). *De-stressing stress: The power of mindsets and the art of stressing mindfully*. In A. N. Le, C. T. Ngnoumen, and E. J. Langer (Eds.), The handbook of mindfulness. Hoboken, NJ: John Wiley & Sons, pp. 948–63.

Csikszentmihalyi, M. (1990). Flow: *The psychology of optimal experience*. New York, NY: Harper-Collins.

Dale, G. A., and Wrisberg, C. A. (1996). The use of a performance profiling technique in a team setting: Getting athletes and coaches on the "same page." *The sport psychologist*, 10, 261–77.

De Jaegher, H. Di Paolo, E., and Gallagher, S. (2010). Can social interaction constitute social cognition? *Trends in Cognitive Sciences*, 14, 441–47. doi:10.1016/j.tics.2010.06.009

Deregowski, J. B., Muldrow, E. S., and Muldrow, W. F. (1972). Pictorial recognition in a remote Ethiopian population. *Perception*, 1(4), 417–425.

DiBerardinis, J. D., Barwind, J., Flanninam, R. R., and Jenkins, V. (1983). Enhanced interpersonal relation as predictor of athletic performance. *International Journal of Sport Psychology*, 14, 243–51.

Fatemi, S. M. (2014). Exemplifying a shift of paradigm: Exploring the psychology of possibility and embracing the instability of knowing the instability of knowing. In A. Le, C. T. Ngoumen, and E. J. Langer (Eds.), *The handbook of mindfulness*. Hoboken, NJ: Wiley, pp. 115–38.

Fineburg, A. (2004). Introducing positive psychology to the introductory psychology student. In P. A. Linley and S. Joseph (Eds.), *Positive psychology in practice*. Hoboken, NJ: John Wiley & Sons.
Fischer, C. T. (2006). *Qualitative research methods for psychologists: Introduction through empirical studies*. San Diego, CA: Academic Press.
Gadamer, H. (1988). *Truth and method*. New York, NY: The Crossroad Publishing Company (Original 1965, 1975 English).
Gardner, F. L., and Moore, Z. E. (2004). A mindfulness-acceptance-commitment-based approach to athletic performance enhancement. *Behavior Therapy*, 35, 707–723.
———. (2006). *Clinical sport psychology*. Champaign, IL: Human Kinetics.
———. (2007). *The psychology of enhancing human performance: The mindfulness-acceptance-commitment (MAC) approach*. New York: Springer.
Glass, D. C., and Singer, J. E. (1972). *Urban stress: Experiments on noise and social stressors*. New York: Academic Press.
Ha'iri Yazdi, M. (1992). *The principles of epistemology in Islamic philosophy*. State University of New York Press.
Hall, T. (1998). Seeking a focus on joy in the field of psychology. *New York Times*, Tuesday April 28, section F, p.7.
Harre, R., and Secord, P. F. (1972). *The explanation of social behavior*. Oxford, UK: Basil Blackwell.
Harvey, J. H., and Weary, G. (1984). Current issues in attribution theory and research. *Annual Review of Psychology*, 35, 427–59.
Heidegger, M. (1959). *An introduction to metaphysics*. New Haven, CT: Yale University Press.
Horwitz, A. V. (2002). *Creating mental illness*. Chicago, IL: University of Chicago Press.
James, W. (1958). *The varieties of religious experience; A study in human nature*. New York, NY: New American Library.
———. (1971). *A pluralistic universe*. In R. B. Perry (Eds.), Essays in radical empiricism and a pluralistic universe. New York, NY: Dutton.
Johnson, W., and Krueger, R. F. (2005). Higher perceived life control decreases genetic variance in physical health: Evidence from a national twin study. *Journal of Personality and Social Psychology*, 88, 165–73.
Kabat-Zinn, J. (2003). *Mindfulness-based Interventions in Context: Past, Present, and Future. Clinical Psychology: Science and Practice*, 10(2), 144–56.
———. (2005). *Coming to Our Senses: Healing Ourselves and the World Through Mindfulness*. New York: Hyperion.
———. (1994). *Wherever you go there you are*. New York: Hyperion.
Kabat-Zinn, J., Beall, B., and Rippe, J. (1985, April). *A systematic mental training program based on mindfulness meditation to optimize performance in collegiate and Olympic rowers*. Paper presented at the World Congress in Sport Psychology, Copenhagen, Denmark.
Kabat-Zinn, J., Lipworth, L., and Burney, R. (1985). The clinical use of mindfulness meditation for the self-regulation of chronic pain. *Journal of Behavioral Medicine*, 8, 163–90.
Kahneman, D. and Frederick, S. (2002). Representativeness revised: Attribute substitution in intuitive judgment. In T. Gilovich, D. Griffin, and D. Kahneman (eds.), *Heuristic and biases: The psychology of intuitive judgement* (pp. 49–81). New York: Cambridge University Press.
Kanfer, F. H. (1970). Self-regulation: Research, issues, and speculations. In C. Neuringer and J. L. Michaels (Eds.), *Behavior modification in clinical psychology*. New York: Appleton-Century-Crofts.
Kelley, H. H., and Michela, J. L. (1980). Attribution theory and research. *Annual Review of Psychology*, 31, 457–501.
Kruglanski, A. W. and Orehek, E. (2007). Partitioning the domain of social influence: Dual Mode and system models and their alternatives. *Annual Review of Psychology*, 58, 291–316.
Kuhn, T. S. (1962). *The structure of scientific revolution*. Chicago, IL: The University of Chicago Press.

Lachman, M. (2006). Perceived control over aging-related declines: Adaptive beliefs and behaviors. *Current Directions in Psychological Sciences*, 15, 282–86.

Langer, E. J. (1989). *Mindfulness*. Reading, MA: Addison-Wesley.

———. (1997). *The power of mindful learning*. Reading, MA: Addison-Wesley.

———. (2000). Mindful learning. *Journal of the American Psychological Society*, 9, 220–22.

———. (2005). *On becoming an artist: Reinventing yourself through mindful creativity*. New York, NY: Ballantine Books.

———. (2009). *Counterclockwise: Mindful health and the power of possibility*. New York, NY: Ballantine Books.

Langer, E. J. and Abelson, R. P. (1974). A patient by any other name . . . : Clinician group difference in labeling bias. *Journal of Consulting and Clinical Psychology*, 42, 4–9.

Langer, E. J., Bashner, R., and Chanowitz, B. (1985). Decreasing prejudice by increasing discrimination. *Journal of Personality and Social Psychology*, 49, 113–20.

Langer, E. J., Blank, A., and Chanowitz, B. (1978). The mindlessness of ostensibly thoughtful action: The role of "placebic" information in interpersonal interaction. *Journal of Personality and Social Psychology*, 36(6), 635–42. doi:10.1037/0022-3514.36.6.635.

Langer, E. J., Carson, S., and Shih, M. (in press). Sit still and pay attention? *Journal of Adult Development*.

Langer E. J., and Rodin, J. (1976). The effects of choice and enhanced personal responsibility for the aged: A field experiment in an institutional setting. *Journal of Personality and Social Psychology*, 34, 191–98.

Lantieri, L., and Goleman, D. P. (2008). *Building emotional intelligence: Techniques to cultivate inner strength in children*. Boulder, CO: Sounds True.

Lausic, D., Tennebaum, G., Eccles, D., Jeong, A. and Johnson, T. (2009). Intrateam communication and performance in double tennis. *Research Quarterly for Exercise and Sport*, 80, 281–90.

Linley, P. A., and Joseph, P. (2004). Toward a theoretical foundation for positive psychology in practice. In P. A. Linley and S. Joseph (Eds.), *Positive psychology in practice*. Hoboken, NJ: John Wiley & Sons.

Lykken, D., andTellegen, A. (1996). Happiness is a stochastic phenomenon. *Psychological Science*, 7, 186–89.

Maddux, J. E., Snyder, C. R., and Lopez, S. (2004). Towards a positive clinical psychology: Deconstructing the illness ideology and constructing an ideology of human strengths and potential. In P. A. Linley and S. Joseph (Eds.), *Positive psychology in practice*. Hoboken, NJ: John Wiley & Sons.

McCrae, R. R., and Costa, P. T. (1990). *Personality in adulthood*. New York, NY: Guilford Press.

Medich, C., Stuart, E., and Chase, S. (1997). Healing through integration: promoting wellness in cardiac rehabilitation. *Journal of Cardiovascular Nursing*, 11(3), 66–79.

Menec, V. H., Chipperfield, J. G., and Perry, R. P. (1999). Self-perceptions of health: A prospective analysis of mortality, control and health. *Journal of Gerontology: Psychological Sciences*, 54B, 85–93.

Nadeau, R. (1991). *Mind, machines and human consciousness*. Chicago, IL: Contemporary Books.

Nelson, G., and Prilleltensky, I. (2005). *Community psychology: In pursuit of liberation and wellbeing*. New York, NY: Palgrave Macmillan.

Parker, I. (1989). *The crisis in modern social psychology, and how to end it*. London, UK: Routledge.

Paul, L., & Weinert, C. (1999). Wellness profile of midlife women with a chronic illness. *Public Health Nursing*, 16(5), 341–50.

Perry, R. P. (2003). Perceived (academic) control and causal thinking in achievement settings. *Canadian Psychology*, 2, 35–49.

Perry, R. P., Hladkyj, S., Pekrun, R. H., and Pelletier, S. T. (2001). Academic control and action control in the achievement of college students. A longitudinal field study, *Journal of Educational Psychology*, 93, 776–89.

Petty, R. E., and Cacioppo, J. T. (1986a). *Communication and persuasion: Central and peripheral routes to attitude change*. New York, NY: Springer-Verlag.

———. (1986b). The elaboration likelihood model of persuasion. In L. Berkowitz (Ed.), *Advances in experimental social psychology* (Vol. 19, pp. 123–205). San Diego, CA: Academic Press.

Regehr, C., Cadell, S., and Jansen, K. (1999). Perceptions of control and long-term recovery from rape. *American Journal of Orthopsychiatry*, 69, 110–15.

Rehm, L. P. (1977). A self control model of depression. *Behavior Therapy*, 8, 787–804.

Ricoeur, P. (1991). *A Ricoeur reader; reflection and imagination*. Toronto: University of Toronto Press.

———. (1991). *From text to action. Essays in hermeneutics*. Illinois: North Western University Press.

Richards, R. (Ed.). (2007). Everyday creativity and new views of human nature: psychological, social and spiritual perspectives. *American Psychological Association*. Washington, DC.

Rodin, J. (1986). Aging and health: Effects of the sense of control. *Science*, 233, 1271–76.

Rodin, J., and Langer, E. (1977). Long-term effects of a control-relevant intervention with the institutionalized aged. *Journal of Personality and Social Psychology*, 35, 897–902.

Rotter, J. B. (1954). *Social learning and clinical psychology*. Englewood Cliffs, NJ: Prentice Hall.

Ruthig, J. C., Haynes, T. L., Stupnisky, R. H., and Perry, R. P. (2009). Perceived academic control: Mediating the effects of optimism and social support on college students' psychological health. *Social Psychology of Education*, 12, 233–49.

Schneider, F. W. Gruman, J. A., and Coutts, L. M. (2012). *Applied social psychology, understanding and addressing social and practical problems*. Oxford University Press.

Schulz, R. (1976). Effects of control and predictability on the physical and psychological well- being of the institutionalized aged. *Journal of Personality and Social Psychology*, 33, 563–73.

Schulz, R., and Hanusa, B. H. (1978). Long- term effects of control and predictability enhancing interventions: Findings and ethical issues. *Journal of Personality and Social Psychology*, 36, 1194–1201.

Scileppi, J. A., Teed, E. L., and Torres, R. D. (2000). *Community psychology, a common sense approach to mental health*. Upper Saddle River, NJ: Prentice-Hall.

Seligman, M. E. P. (2002). *Authentic happiness: Using the new positive psychology to realize your potential for lasting fulfillment*. New York, NY: Free Press.

Seligman, M. E. P., and Csikszentmihalyi, M. (Eds.). (2000). Positive psychology. *American Psychologist*, 55(1), 5–14.

Skinner, E. A. (1995). *Perceived control, motivation and coping*. Thousand Oaks, CA: Sage.

Smith, R. A., Wallston, B. S., Wallston, K. A., Forsberg, P. R., and King, J. E. (1984). Measuring desire for control of health care processes. *Journal of Personality and Social Psychology*, 47, 415–26.

Sorrentino, R. M. (2003). Motivated perception and the warm look: current perspectives and future directions. In S. J. Spencer, S. Fein, M. P. Zanna, and J. M. Olson Eds.), *Motivated social perception: The Ontario symposium*, Vol. 9, pp. 299–316. Mahwah, NJ: Erlbaum.

Sorrentino, R. M., and Higgins, E. T. (1986). *Motivation and cognition: Warming to synergism*. In R. M. Sorrentino and E. T. Higgins (Eds.), The handbook of motivation and cognition: foundations of social behavior (pp. 3–19). New York: Guilford.

Spariosu, M. I. (2004). *Global intelligence and human development: toward an ecology of global learning*. Cambridge: The MIT Press.

Sporer, S. L., Trinkl, B., and Guberova, E. (2007). Matching faces: differences in processing speed of out-group faces by different groups. *Journal of Cross-Cultural Psychology*, 38, 398–412.

Suh, E. M., Diener-E., and Fujita, F. (1996). Event and subjective well-being: Only recent events matter. *Journal of Personality and Social Psychology*, 70, 1091–1102.

Sullivan, P. J. (1995). The relationship between communication and cohesion in inter-collegiate rugby players (Unpublished master's thesis). University of Windsor, Ontario, Canada.
Sullivan, P. and Feltz, D. L. (2003). The preliminary development of the Scale for Effective Communication in Sport Teams (SECTS). *Journal of Applied Social Psychology*, 33, 1693-1715. doi: 10.1111/j.1559-1816.2003.tb01970.x
Thompson, S. C. (1981). Will it hurt less if I can control it? A complex answer to a simple question. *Psychological Bulletin*, 90, 89–101.
Thompson, J. K., and Heinberg, L. J. (1999). The media's influence on body image disturbance and eating disorders: We've reviled them, now can we rehabilitate them? *Journal of Social Issues*, 55, 339–53.
Topolski, D. (1989). *True blue: The story of the Oxford boat race mutiny*. London: Bantam Books.
VanderStoep, S. W., Fagerlin, A., and Feenstra, J. S. (2000). What do students remember from introductory psychology? *Teaching of Psychology*, 2, 89–92.
Wallston, B. S., and Wallston, K. A. (1981). Health locus of control. In H. Lefcourt (Ed.), *Research with the locus of control construct* (Vol. I). New York: Academic Press.
———. (1984). Social psychological models of health behavior: An examination and interaction. In A. Baum, S. Taylor, and J. E. Singer (Eds.), Handbook of psychology and health: Vol. V. *Social aspects of health*. Hillsdale, NJ: Erlbaum.
Wallston, K. A., and Wallston, B. S. (1982). Who is responsible for your health? The construct of health locus of control. In G. Sanders and J. M. Suls (Eds.), *Social psychology of health and illness*. Hillsdale, NJ: Erlbaum.
Wilson, E. O. (1998). *Consilience: The unity of knowledge*. London, UK: Little, Brown.
Woolgar, S. (1988). *Science: The very idea*. Chichester, UK: Ellis Horwood.
Zajonc, R. B. (1984). On the primacy of affect. *American Psychologist,* 39, 117–23.
Zenner, C., Herrnleben-Kurz, S., Walatch, H. (2014). Mindfulness-based interventions in schools- a systematic review and meta-analysis. *Frontiers in Psychology,* 5,603.
Zoogman, S., Goldberg, S., Hoyt, W., Miller, L. (2014). Mindfulness interventions with youth. A meta-analysis. *Mindfulness,* 6 (2), 1–13.

INDEX

ABOUT THE AUTHOR

Sayyed Mohsen Fatemi, PhD, is affiliated with Ferdowsi University of Mashhad, Mashhad, Iran, as an associate professor of psychology and the chair of the Desk of North America. He completed his post-doctoral studies in the Department of Psychology at Harvard University, where he also served as a teaching fellow, an associate, and a fellow.

Dr. Fatemi works on mindfulness and its psychological implications for cross-cultural, clinical, and social psychology. He is the author of numerous books and has had articles published in journals such as the American Psychological Association (APA) *Journal of Theoretical and Philosophical Psychology*.

He has published numerous works, including his new book, *The Psychological Power of Language*. He is also the recipient of the Ellen Langer International mindfulness award.

www.ingramcontent.com/pod-product-compliance
Ingram Content Group UK Ltd.
Pitfield, Milton Keynes, MK11 3LW, UK
UKHW041122071026
15587UKWH00009B/73

9 781498 574228